Heading for Oregon

*Living in a Sod House
Beside the Oregon Trail*

Clara Kirkpatrick Lau

Foreword by Dan Dunkelberger
and Beverly Maloy

AuthorHouse™
1663 Liberty Drive
Bloomington, IN 47403
www.authorhouse.com
Phone: 1-800-839-8640

© *2009 Clara Kirkpatrick Lau. All rights reserved.*

No part of this book may be reproduced, stored in a retrieval system, or transmitted by any means without the written permission of the author.

First published by AuthorHouse 5/13/2009

ISBN: 978-1-4389-4348-0 (sc)

Printed in the United States of America
Bloomington, Indiana

This book is printed on acid-free paper.

STORIES OF OUR LIFE
ON THE NORTH PLATTE VALLEY

By
Clara Kirkpatrick Lau

Table of Contents

Foreword by	Daniel Dunkelberger and Beverly Maloy	ix
Memories	A Poem	xi
Chapter 1	Leaving Kansas-Heading for Oregon	1
Chapter 2	Arrival on the North Platte River Valley	13
Chapter 3	The Storm While Living in a Tent	22
Chapter 4	Building Our Sod House	28
Chapter 5	Fire!	39
Chapter 6	Thanksgiving Turkey	50
Chapter 7	Christmas	58
Chapter 8	The Ridgepole in the Sod House	71
Chapter 9	Deer Hunt	75
Chapter 10	Father's Illness	83
Chapter 11	Riding Jack, the Bay Mule	86
Chapter 12	Eddie and the Rattle Snake	90
Chapter 13	Willis Court and His Eye for the Girls	96
Chapter 14	The Day Lighting Struck Zena Dead!	99
Chapter 15	Hattie Shot!	102

Chapter 16	Tom Wagoner	106
Chapter 17	Frank and the Rattler!	110
Chapter 18	School Days	115
Chapter 19	The Move to Sidney	124
Chapter 20	The Mail that Brought Good Cheer!	127
Chapter 21	On To Oregon! (1890)	133

Foreword by

Daniel Dunkelberger and Beverly Maloy

With computer on hand and a great desire to have this book published I give you the story of Clara Kirkpatrick Lau.

This book was written by our great aunt many years ago. It was left in the hands of Daniel, who with his wife Rebekah, researched many of the homesteads where the Kirkpatrick's had lived that are mentioned in this book.

Rebekah is the illustrator of this book's cover giving us a scene of what she has imagined it to be like when the Kirkpatrick's were preparing to leave Lenore, Kansas and head for Oregon.

Our sole purpose of this book is to give the families of this era a look into their past, and see the struggles of their ancestors who had such a strong Spirit of God and courage to take on the task of leaving home, family and friends to head west to an unseen land and unknown future to start a new life.

With God's grace they were able to accomplish that goal.

MEMORIES

Oh, don't you remember, sweet mother of mine
The days that we spent near the Platte River pine;
The house that we had that was made out of sod
And the heart-scenes that still
draw us nearer to God?

And do you remember that rollick some brood
Who always were noisy, but never were rude,
Who chattered and prattled and giggled and cried,
But who, after all, were real humans inside?

And do you remember the jolly, good dad
Who loved us and spanked us
and then made us glad.
By telling us stories and singing us songs
Till we forgot all our spankings and
he forgot all our wrongs?

Can't you see him now in the firelight glow
When winter was flinging her billows of snow
With a kid on each knee and the rest on the floor
How we laughed at his jingles
and begged him for more?

See the dear elder brother, more dignified grown
And your own precious self sitting near, looking on
How we listened and laughed at
his rollick some rhymes
Till we hear them in memories thousands of times?

Chapter 1

Leaving Kansas-Heading for Oregon

The corn leaves rustled lazily in the breeze as Joe Kirkpatrick strode down the long rows. The sound was music in his ears and he whistled a low accompaniment.

The best crop I've had in years, he was thinking and he fell to estimating the profits the eighty acres of corn would mean to him and his family when in the fall it was harvested and sold. "I can finish paying for the house and for the new mower I bought yesterday," he told himself. "Libby can have a new dress and the children can have good clothes to wear to school."

His ruddy complexion and black, curly hair gave the impression of middle-aged manhood. He was fifty, though he did not look it. Three years of military training in the Civil War had resulted in an erect bearing and elasticity of step seldom seen in a man of his age, especially a western farmer who had fought the elements for a living for so many years. His alert brown eyes took in the beauty of the long, straight rows. "Like soldiers on parade," he mused.

"Hey, Dad!" called a cheery voice as Joe glanced up to see his nineteen year old son, Will, perched on the high seat of the new mower, his lithe body poised as if on a racing saddle. His dark brown eyes glowed under a shock of straight, black hair that showed beneath a battered, brown felt hat. The bay horses switched their tails at flies and cropped the heads of the tall, ripe grass along the edge of the hayfield.

"Hey, yourself and see how you like it!" his father replied and stepped briskly out to where the mower stood. He had become so absorbed in estimating the value of the corn crop that he had forgotten they were to try out the new mower that morning.

"How do you like the new machine?" he asked.

"She works like a top," replied Will. "I've cut a swath around the barnyard. Want to try it?"

"Sure thing!" replied Joe. "Get down and I'll take a whack at it. I've been looking at the corn," he continued. "It's the finest crop we've had since we came west. I hope nothing happens to it before we can get it harvested and sold. Two years ago the drought took the crop and last year it was the grasshoppers. If anything happens to this crop I'm goin' to leave the country. It'll be 'Westward Ho!' for this family."

Joe mounted the seat of the mower, clucked to the horses and drove around the hayfield, just to try out the new machine. He found it as satisfactory as he had hoped. Will was sitting in the narrow shade of a corn hill when Joe returned.

"Some shade!" Will remarked, "but better than none on a day like this."

"We'll leave the mower here and come out in the wagon after dinner," Joe said. "That hay's just right to cut now."

They unhitched the horses, mounted them and rode to the stable. There they tossed hayforks, a hammer, a box of nails and some wrenches into the wagon-box.

"A man never knows what he may need with a new machine," Joe remarked as he threw the last tool into the box.

"Gee! I wish it'd rain!" exclaimed Will, wiping the perspiration from his forehead with his shirt sleeve. "This heat gets me."

"Don't wish for rain now," his father replied, "not until after that hay's in. A good shower wouldn't hurt the corn, but it can wait. It's doing well, couldn't be better," he said proudly.

Dinner was on the big table in the kitchen, Joe's wife, Libby, sat on the doorstep waiting; her slight figure drooped perceptibly with weariness. The heat was almost too much for her frail strength. Beads of perspiration stood on her white forehead where a few auburn locks rested damply.

"How's Mother?" Will asked as he took the steps two at a time.

"Fine," replied his mother. "Dinner's ready."

Joe stooped and kissed the pale cheek. "We're ready, too," he said, "and as hungry as bears."

"Come, children!" called Libby, and five robust youngsters ranging in age from two to eleven years came trooping in from as many different directions and seated themselves at the table. There was no crowding or pushing. Joe and Libby had taught their children better manners than that.

Joe took his place at the head of the table. Libby sat at the opposite end with Eddie on her lap. She couldn't trust him to be a little gentleman yet. He was too young, this red-headed, round-faced dumpling of a baby. He covered his eyes with his pudgy fingers while Joe asked the blessing, but just as it was finished he shouted, "Amen! Taters, Taters!"

"No! No!" his mother admonished. The rest of the children giggled.

"You rascal!" grinned Joe. "You must be hungry, too!"

Dinner was soon over and Joe and Will were in the hayfield at work. The wagon stood at the edge of the field where it would be handy in case a tool was needed. The air was hot and sultry and a blue-gray haze lay across the hills to the west. The blades of corn hung limp in the merciless heat. Not a living creature was in sight, not even a lizard or a ground squirrel, for all had sought some cooler spot where they could breathe in comfort.

Libby finished the family wash she had started before dinner. As she carried the heavy basket of clothes to the line she noticed a dark cloud forming in the western sky. "Could that mean rain?" she wondered. She hoped not, for the hay harvest had just begun. She moved swiftly from basket to line as she hung the clothes to dry. The heat made her feel faint. "They'll dry in a few minutes," she said as she hung the last garment on the line.

She swung the basket lightly by the handle as she started to the house, humming an old tune, one that she and her sisters had sung when they were children together. It brought back memories of her girlhood and of the family as they were in those bygone days.

Their mother, a descendent of an old and cultured family, had died when Libby was six years old. Her father had married again and still lived in the old home in western Missouri. A circuit judge of the old school, he had spent much of his time in the saddle, riding from courthouse to courthouse, and holding court for the people of the surrounding country.

Of the six little girls of the family Libby was next to the eldest. All were living except the youngest sister who had died since Libby came west. Her other sisters were all grown and married now, and she had many nieces and nephews whom she had never seen. How she longed to see them all! She had even dared hope that if the corn crop turned out well this year they might make a trip back home to visit them. One sister, Lena, had gone to Oregon when in her teens and was living there with her husband and three daughters.

She stopped short as she rounded the corner of the house. There was an ominous stillness that she had not noticed before. She sensed impending danger. The black cloud in the western sky, which had been no bigger than a man's hat when she came out, was now a great, black thunderhead which hung like a ball of ebony in the murky sky. A gust of wind lifted small clouds of dust and sent them skyward in slender, spiraling dust-devils. The cloud grew perceptibly larger as she watched it, and the wind began carrying it down the valley at terrific speed. Streaks of chain lightning flashed across the face of the clouds followed by sharp peals of thunder rented the air.

Libby turned quickly, clothes-basket in hand, and hurried back to the line. The wind was blowing with steadily increasing velocity. The wash-tub which she had left half-full of water outside the kitchen door was upset and the water was splashed about the dooryard. Chicken-coops were overturned and the chickens were fluttering to the stable, their tails spread out like fans. As Libby tugged frantically at the last sheet on the line, hailstones the size of teacups began to fall. There were only a few at first, each one giving out a thud like apples falling on dry ground.

She hurried into the house, set the basket of clothes on the kitchen floor and ran out to close the shutters. The windows would be smashed to bits if the shutters were left open. Running into the house she closed and bolted the door, then looked about to see if all the children were there. One of those hailstones could kill a child if it struck him on the head. The children were in the house. They had seen western storms before and didn't care to be out in one of them. Eleven year old Lizzie had the two younger children-- Hattie, four, and Eddie, two, on the bed in the corner of the living room. She had made a little tent from a quilt and the three were huddled together under it.

Stella and Clara had been flattening their noses against the windowpane, watching the storm approach. They covered their eyes with their hands whenever the lightning flashed. The thunder reminded them of Rip Van Winkle and the Men-of-the-Mountains playing ten pin. When their mother slammed the shutter they dodged back with a shriek, thinking the lightning had struck the house. When Libby came in they were standing in the middle of the floor with their arms about each other laughing hysterically; then bursting into tears they ran to their mother and buried their faces in her gingham skirt. She put her arms about them and led them to the bed where Lizzie and the two younger children had taken refuge.

Leaving the five children on the bed Libby stepped to the east window and looked out toward the hayfield. She could see the wagon standing at the edge of the field. The horses were unhitched from the mower and tied to the wagon with their backs to the storm. Tails switching in the wind and heads down, they were patiently taking the beating the hail was giving them. She could see two figures under the wagon where Joe and Will had taken refuge from the storm, she could not see the mower, but hoped her husband and son were not near it. The steel sickle might attract the electricity.

Suddenly the wind died down to a mere breeze. The hail and rain gradually ceased falling and a great mass of clouds scudded eastward. Streaks of lightning still flashed across the sky and blasts of thunder roared. Farther and farther the clouds drifted, fainter and fainter grew the sound of thunder and flashes of lightning, and the storm had passed as swiftly as it had come.

Joe and Will crawled from under the wagon and looked about them. The tall grass of the hayfield lay flat on the ground as if a tornado had swept over it. "We'll never in the world be able to cut that," said Joe. They examined the horses and found them all right except for a few welts left by the hail.

"Let's go over and take a look at the corn," said Joe. "I wonder what the hail has done to it." Father and son walked across the strip of meadow to the cornfield, brushing the drops of water from the grass as they passed. As they neared the cornfield they could see nothing but the tall, slender canes, where but a few minutes before lush stalks of corn had marched in long, straight rows down the full length of the field with their slender, tapering leaves rustling in the breeze, the tassels just appearing at the tops of the stalks.

Joe stopped, dumfounded. He brushed his hand across his eyes and looked again. Was he seeing straight? For a long moment he stood in dismay. Could this be his precious field of corn? He was not mistaken, scarcely a leaf or a tassel remained on the bare stalks, many of which were twisted and broken. Hailstones lay in win rows between the rows of broken stalks. The corn crop upon which he had depended for his winter's support was gone!

Will looked at his father in silence and pity. His usually erect form seemed bent and old. The black, curly hair appeared not to belong to the drawn, ashen face which so recently was ruddy and smiling.

Without a word they walked back to the wagon. Silently they hitched up the team and climbed to the green wooden seat. Joe took the reins mechanically and drove to the stable. They unhitched the horses and tied them in their stalls, then strode silently to the house, Will's arm across the shoulders of his father.

Joe must talk it over with Libby. Perhaps they together could find a way out. There must be a way out! That evening a little prayer service was held around the family alter and Joe prayed for guidance in solving the problems of his misfortune. Then he led his family with a quavering voice in his favorite hymn:

> I know my Heavenly Father knows
> The storms that would my way oppose.

That night he and Libby talked long and earnestly about the whole sickening situation. It seemed impossible to stay on where crops failed year after year. The drought, the grasshoppers and now the hail had done their deadly work.

"A man has no right to keep a family in a place like this!" he told Libby: "no churches, school three miles away and the house we'll never be able to pay for it with every source of income cut off!"

Libby knew that he was right. "We must trust in God and do the best we can," she said.

Morning dawned clear and bright. The earth was refreshed by yesterday's rain and Joe's spirits had risen from the dark abyss into which the loss of his hay and corn crops had plunged him. A resolute look was in his dark eyes as he stood by the kitchen window gazing out over the level prairie to the west.

"Oregon!" the name kept ringing in his ear, "Oregon, the land that floweth with milk and honey!"

"Libby," he said, turning from the window, "when we sold out in Ohio we thought we would go to Oregon, but then there was the prospect of getting cheap land here in Kansas. I came here and homesteaded this piece of rich, level land and built this house out of that soft, yellow magnesia stone from the gull on the back of the place. It didn't cost much and it has made us a good, warm house, but I didn't have cash enough to pay for labor and other materials, so, as you know, I borrowed money and gave a mortgage on the place, then went back to Ohio for you and the children. It all took money, but I hoped to pay out in a few years. Now, the money is gone; the corn crop is gone and all we have left is the team and wagon with a few chickens and a cow and some pigs. Even the new mower's not all paid for and the hay's as flat as a pancake. It never can be cut. It's fit only for pasture when there's no snow on the ground. If I had only myself to think of, it wouldn't be so bad, but here are you and the six children to take into consideration. Something must be done for the family. We are this far on our way to Oregon. Let's go on, Libby, to where we can at least make a living."

And so they decided to make the long trek to Oregon.

Early the next spring of 1887 the claim was sold, not for as much as Joe thought it should bring, but enough to outfit them with a good team of mules, a covered wagon and some money; enough, Joe thought, to supply their needs until they reached Oregon and got settled. There was much to be done, so there was no time to be lost.

The furniture had been sold with the house, and a sale was held to get rid of the farm machinery. Everything was now in readiness for packing and moving. Joe added a foot board to the top of the wagon box to provide more storage space. He built a partition across the back of the box and made a trap-door to cover it. "This will be a good place for cooking utensils," he said. He built a floor to be laid even with the top of the wagon box, leaving room in the lower compartment for storage of such articles as would not be needed until they reached their destination.

From the wall in the living room he removed the big Welsh clock. "We'll pack this under the floor of the wagon box," he said. "We have the alarm clock that we can use on the road."

"That's my clock," said Clara, her tow head thrown back proudly, her brown eyes watching her father eagerly.

"Yes," said Joe. "It was bought on the day you were born and has ticked off every second of your life to this very minute. I'll wrap it in this blue and white coverlid my mother wove on her handloom before I was born. We must take good care of both of them."

The big Dutch oven with its heavy lid was packed in the space in the back of the wagon under the trap door, to be convenient when we need it, "Libby said. "I can bake enough biscuits for the whole family in that." The Dutch oven was a large cast-iron pan with four short legs and a heavy iron cover and a bail with which to lift it.

Yards and yards of heavy canvas were bought from which Libby made a tent for the family to sleep in while on the road. Will built a food box which he strapped to the side of the wagon, then a large chest for bedding. "This can be nailed to the side of the wagon," he said, viewing his handiwork with pride. Bedding was sorted, folded neatly and packed in the chest. Will filled a bed thick with hay and placed it in the wagon box where his mother and the three younger children were to sleep. A sheet was to be hung across the middle of the tent. Joe and Will were to sleep on one side of the tent and Lizzie and

Clara on the other. A small sheet iron cook stove was purchased. This was so light that one of the older girls could lift it with ease. It was packed in the wagon box where it could be easily reached.

"All set?" called Joe from his perch on the high wagon seat on the morning they were ready to start.

"Yes, the children are all here," answered Libby from the back seat. Clara and Lizzie sat beside her, their feet dangling in mid-air, while the three younger children, Stella, Hattie and Eddie, romped on the floor of the wagon. Frank, the black and tan shepherd dog looked on wistfully, wagging his tail. He was ready to follow wherever the family might lead.

"Come on, old fellow," called Will and the dog took his place between the rear wheels of the wagon.

"Ho, for Oregon!" shouted Will, as he climbed to the seat beside his father. He cracked the whip over the mules' backs. Jack, his bay coat glistening in the morning sunlight, threw his weight against his collar, but Pete, the brown mule, laid back his ears and refused to budge.

"Go on, you rascal!" urged Will, toughing the brown coat lightly with the whip. Startled, the mule gave a lurch and reached Jack's side.

"Steady, there!" Joe called, drawing the reins taut, and in a few minutes both mules were pulling together and Joe Kirkpatrick and his family was on their long journey to Oregon.

Libby prayed that they reach their destination in safety.

Chapter 2

Arrival on the North Platte River Valley

It was late evening when the travelers reached the sod house where John Fisk with his wife and two children lived. The long twilight, so familiar to prairie dwellers was merging into darkness. Joe had been told about the Fisks while he was in North Platte city. The man at the feed stable where Joe had gone to buy oats for the mules told him about them.

"They're the doggondest, finest folks you ever see anywhere. No money to speak of but plenty of good sense and real, honest-to-goodness friendliness. They went out there two years ago and took up a claim. Livin' in a sod house they say and as happy as larks."

The covered wagon creaked to a stop in front of the crude dwelling and Joe climbed down from the high seat. A big shepherd dog greeted him with a friendly bark, wagging his bushy tail. Frank, Joe's dog, sniffed at him and seemed satisfied that he was a good neighbor. A middle-aged man appeared in the deep-set doorway of the sod house, his sturdy form silhouetted against the light from a kerosene lamp on the table behind him.

"Well, I'll be jiggered!" exclaimed a friendly voice. "If it ain't a kivered wagon and a passel of kids. Git the lantern, Billy, an' let's see what it's all about."

A tall, lanky boy of sixteen went to bring the lantern, his bare feet scuffing on the loose sand of the dooryard, making a sound like a flock of sheep running over dry grass.

John Fisk didn't wait for the lantern. In a matter of minutes he and Joe were chatting like old friends.

"Come in!" he urged. "Don't keep the woman and them kids cooped up in a wagon when there's lots of room in the house."

Libby gave one glance at the tiny house and bit her lip to keep from smiling. How could he expect a tribe like that to get inside so small a house?

"We have our camping outfit," said Joe. "All we need is a place to pitch our tent and some water for ourselves and the mules. We can manage the rest."

"Naw, come on in an' meet the Missus," objected Fisk.

"I would like to meet your wife," said Libby. "We heard such fine things about all of you in North Platte."

The angular form of Mrs. Fisk appeared in the door of a tent which was pitched near the house. Peering through the semi-darkness she queried, "Who is it, John?" and straining her eyes to see she continued, "Bring 'em in the house."

As Libby neared the door of the tent she heard a girlish voice coming through the darkness.

"Have you wished tonight? Have you wished tonight?" droned the voice as of one in delirium.

"No, not yet," answered the mother. Then turning to Libby she explained, "Hattie, our girl, is mighty sick. She's out of her head most of the time. We think she drunk some water from one of them alkali ponds down toward the river. There's a white rim of alkali all around the edge of the ponds an' the water tastes bitter and slimy. She shouldn't have drunk it. She's better now, but she's still out of her head. Ever since we come here the kids has made a wish on the stars every night. That's what she meant by wishin'."

"Star light, star bright, the first star I've seen tonight," the girlish voice trailed off into silence.

The mother completed the sentence, "I wish I may, I wish I might have the wish I wish tonight."

"Yes, that's it," murmured the girl and turned her face to the wall of the tent.

"Now, she'll go to sleep," said the mother. "She has to have her wish every night before she'll sleep. Where'd you'll come from?" she inquired abruptly.

Libby told her briefly of their journey: how they had come from western Kansas and had traveled for three weeks. "We're on our way to Oregon," she told Mrs. Fisk, "but it's such a long, hard trip we think we'll sell our team and wagon when we reach Cheyenne, Wyoming and go the rest of the way by train."

"That's a hundred miles or more from here," said Mrs. Fisk, "anit's gittin hotter and hotter every day. Too hot to travel in a wagon."

"We may not go that far before we take the train," said Libby.

John Fisk's big voice was booming from outside where he and Joe stood, Joe leaning against the wagon wheel and Fisk, with elbows akimbo near him, his hands thrust deep into overalls pockets. "It's the purtiest country you ever seen," he said. "Jist pitch your tent right over thar in that patch of grass an' help yourself to water. There's plenty of it in this twenty foot well an' in the mornin' when it's good an' daylight you'll drive right through the place I've been tellin' you about an' you'll say I'm no liar. I wish now I'd have gone there before I filed on this claim. It ain't bad here, but that sure is a humdinger, especially at this time of year when the grass is at its best. It's like a green carpet all over the valley."

The dew was still on the grass when the travelers started on their way the next morning. Joe Kirkpatrick and John Fisk shook hands. Libby and the girls said goodbye to Mrs. Fisk.

"I hope your daughter is better," said Libby.

"She is better," said the mother. "I think it done her good to hear voices around the place."

The two older boys were still talking when the family was ready to start. They talked of guns and grouse and prairie chickens and of deer and antelope that roamed the hills on either side of the great river that rolled between the ranges.

"Well, son, let's go," called Joe. "We may see these folks again, but we must be on our way now."

The two boys shook hands and Will took his shotgun which he had been showing to Billy. "I'll go on ahead, Dad," he said. "Maybe I'll find a grouse or something for dinner."

"Okay," replied his father, "but keep an eye on the covered wagon. There's no telling where we'll be by noon."

Joe thanked Mr. Fisk for the privilege of camping in their yard and for the hospitalities shown them, shook hands the second time and was again on his way to Oregon.

The long afternoon drew to a close. Lizzie and Clara trudged wearily behind the covered wagon, leaving their footprints in the dusty road.

"Look out for rattlesnakes along the side of the road," warned their mother from the seat beside her husband. Joe flicked the whip over the backs of the mules as they snatched at the heads of the tall grass along the roadside.

Stella sat between her father and mother, her dark, curly head resting on her mother's lap. She slept fitfully as the wagon jolted along. Hattie and Eddie were asleep in the back of the wagon after bouncing around in it during the whole long day.

From North Platte city they had followed the Oregon Trail, and such a road: Cut by thousands of iron wheels of countless wagons, crumbled by the hoofs of herds of cattle which had been driven from Texas and other southern states to pasture lands in the mountains to the west; swept by tireless wind for half a century, the road lay several feet below the level of the surrounding country. The road bed, if it could be called a road bed, was piled inches deep with loose sand.

Suddenly a turn in the road brought into view a landscape that lay like a dream world before them. Stretching in endless waves, a sea of grass lay in undulating folds stirred by a gentle breeze that cause it to rise and fall in the light of the setting sun. At a low place in the bank of the road Joe turned the mules into the most gigantic hayfield he had ever seen. He slackened the reins and the mules ate greedily of the luscious grass while he and Libby gazed in wonder at its beauty.

"Here's where we stay for the night," said Libby.

"Here's where we stay for the rest of our lives," exclaimed Joe. "Did you ever see such grass?"

He climbed down from the wagon seat and examined the grass. It was not very tall and had a loose head made up of smaller heads, each with a slender stem with seeds hanging down on the side of it.

"This is called grama grass," said Joe. "Fisk told me about it last night. He says it makes the finest kind of feed for horses and other stock. It is as good as grain and here it grows as thick as the hair on a dog's back."

The sudden stopping of the wagon awoke the two children in the back of the wagon and they climbed up to the seat with their mother. Stella rubbed her sleepy eyes and sat up. Lizzie and Clara came running to their father to see what had happened.

At that moment Will came up the road with two prairie chickens slung over his shoulder, the blood still dripping from their wrung necks.

"I went down to the river," he said. "That's where I found the birds. If it hadn't been for Frank I'd have lost the last one I shot. He found it in the tall grass. There's a cattle trail down to a low place along the bank. We can drive down there. The ground is level and there's a good camping place by the river."

"Well, let's get going," said Joe. "It's nearly dark and in this country night comes on suddenly. All hands pile in and let's go."

Libby climbed into the wagon and the three little ones scrambled after her with Lizzie and Clara following.

The River – the North Platte River of which they had heard so much was at its best, rolling with majestic grandeur, swollen with the melting snows of the Rocky Mountains in which it had its source. It surged and tumbled as though great giants were underneath its waves pushing and crowding to boost the current along.

The wagon came to a halt a short distance from its margin on a low, grassy plain and preparations were made for camping.

The sun was setting behind the western hills. The wind had ceased to blow and a great calm pervaded the valley. To their left rose a low range of sand hills sparsely covered with scrub pines at the top. To the right another low range crept westward as far as the eye could see, while at their feet the sparkling waters of the river almost a mile in width at that point, glimmered like a silver ribbon as it stretched out of sight. Up the river to the west rose a range of blue hills silhouetted against the ruddy sky and two basaltic pillars loomed out of the prairie floor.

"Those hills are Scott's Bluffs," said Joe, pointing westward, "and that farther shaft that looms up between them and the river is called Courthouse Rock. The tall one this side of it is Chimney Rock. If you look carefully you can see that it has ragged top.

It was once pointed like a church spire, but during the Indian trouble the soldiers that were stationed at Camp Clark by the river above here got hilarious one day and shot the top off from it with a cannon. Fisk told me about that, too. There's a bridge across the North Platte river at Camp Clark."

"A few miles to the west of here is a stream called Cedar Creek, continued Joe. "It empties into the river not far from here. On Cedar Creek, a few miles from the river, is a big cattle ranch. It is run by a man by the name of Radcliffe. Fisk says he is a mighty fine fellow."

"Bring on the chickens," called Joe as he took the big tin pail and started to the river for water.

Lizzie and Clara each had a prairie chicken and were plucking the feathers. Will drew the canvas tent from its hiding place in the wagon and began untying the ropes that held it together. Libby took the little sheet iron stove from moorings at the back of the wagon and carried it to a convenient place while Stella scrambled after the Dutch oven which was in the wagon. It was all she could carry, but she managed to land it safely in a good place near the stove. Hattie and Eddie scampered here and there among the tall grasses, picking up sticks with which to build a fire. Wood was brought from the river bank where it had been carried by the stream and had dried in the hot sun.

"Good for you," said Libby, as the children brought their treasures. "You are Mother's little helpers."

"Fried chicken, yum, yum!" exclaimed Will. "This won't be the last we'll have if we stay around here.

There are thousands of them in this hayfield. I scared up a lot of the young ones, too. You ought to see them run!"

"We will see them in time," said Joe," and we'll have a feast every day."

"I hope you didn't kill the mother hens," said Libby.

"No, these are both roosters," said Will.

"Cock-a-doodle-doo!" crowed Eddie. "I find one rooster fedder!"

The evening meal was soon ready: fried chicken and hot biscuits which Libby had baked in the Dutch oven and plum leather cooked to a pulp while the chickens were frying. A pot of coffee simmered on the coals where the Dutch oven had stood.

Chapter 3

The Storm While Living in a Tent

All day long the sun's rays poured down in merciless heat. Amber haze hung in steaks about the murky sky and at evening the sun plunged its fiery sphere into the sea of animated dust atoms and shot its gleaming streamers toward the zenith. The gramma grass and the gray green willows drooped and hung lifeless as though hoping for a breath, just one brief draught of cool, refreshing air. Even the canvas tent that stood by the river seemed to feel the heat. About its skeleton frame of poles the canvas drooped and hung lifeless in the dead calm.

Joe and Libby sat at the door of the tent on collapsible camp stools, while the five younger children sprawled on the grass, trying to absorb as much coolness as possible from the dry earth. Will had already gone to bed in the covered wagon. Frank, the dog, lay at Joe's feet, his red tongue dripping moisture as he panted for a cool breath.

"This is sure a weather breeder," remarked Joe, whisking the perspiration from his brow with his shirt sleeve. "If it doesn't rain before tomorrow night I'll miss my guess."

Libby sat in uncomfortable silence, watching the amber sky where the sun had dipped out of sight less than an hour before. Suddenly she pointed to the west. "See that black cloud," she said. "It's no bigger than the Dutch oven." The children looked, and then lolled again on the soft grass.

"Just as I thought," said Joe, "rain before tomorrow night."

"Rain before morning, I predict," said Libby. "I hope it doesn't storm while we're living in the tent."

"If it holds off for another week we'll be in the new sod house," replied Joe.

The moon rose up from a sea of blood. The crickets and the katydids hummed faintly from the river's bank, but no breath of air stirred.

"Come, Hattie and Stella! It's time little folks were in bed," said Libby, as she lifted Eddie's sleeping form from the grass at her feet. "It's cooler in the tent now and I hope we can all have a good night's rest."

She entered the tent door with the sleeping child in her arms, removed his clothes except the little undershirt and laid him on the bed without covering him. The two girls were soon undressed and lay sprawling on their bed. "You won't need any covers until later in the night," Libby told them. Then she stepped to the back of the tent, raised the sagging wall and placed a camp stool under it. A cool breeze might in time find its way through the tent and relieve the sleeping children. Libby then lay down beside them, too weary to undress.

Joe still sat by the tent door, watching the black cloud which had grown perceptibly larger since Libby had discovered it. "Come, girls!" he called to his two elder daughters, "time to roll in."

"It's too hot in the tent," protested Lizzie. "It'll be cooler in there in another hour."

"And besides," chimed in Clara, "I want to watch that cloud grow. It gets bigger every minute."

"You're right," agreed Joe. "It's puffing up like a balloon, but I'm too tired to sit up any longer. Slinging sod for a house is no easy job. Good night!" and he disappeared through the tent door.

Frank started up, whining as Joe left him. "Come here, old fellow," called Clara. The dog trotted toward her and lay down beside her as she stroked his velvety ears.

It was past midnight when Libby awoke with a start. The wind was blowing a gale and the tent shook. She lay listening for a moment. A fiercer note in the sound of the wind alarmed her, and such a wind! There was nothing to stop its sweep and it hit the tent with the force that a hurricane hits a liner in mid ocean.

Libby got up and went to the tent door. The moon was shining brightly, casting a silver sheen over the world of green grass stretching to the hills to the west and south and as far east as she could see under its mellow light. To the west she could see a snarl of clouds along the skyline. They seemed twisted into a tangled skein of thread that a kitten had been playing with.

Libby watched the clouds for a few minutes as they marshaled themselves into one solid line and swept up from the horizon like troops forming a battle line. The moon was descending the western sky and soon hid itself behind the cloud mass. The sky above was still aglow with the light.

Libby went back into the tent and lay down beside Joe. She hated to waken him just because she was afraid of a western storm. She dozed off to sleep for a few brief moments, and then awakening suddenly found herself trembling from head to foot. Libby rose and walked quietly to the tent door, trying not to disturb anyone. She could feel the cool wind blowing in on her face. She stepped outside the tent door and closed the flap after her. The wind whipped her long, auburn tresses about her delicately featured face and flattened her white muslin nightgown against her slender body. She had to lean forward to make any advance against it.

By this time the black army of the heavens had rolled up overhead and a few drops of rain had begun to fall, making a little hissing sound in the dust as falling pebbles might do.

Libby ran into the tent. She shook Joe's arm. "Wake up, Joe," she whispered, trying not to disturb and frighten the children. "There's a storm coming up. It's beginning to rain already!"

"Let'er rain!" replied Joe, sleepily. "Rain won't hurt us. The tent's waterproof, I guess."

Libby insisted, "But this is a real storm, Joe. We'd better be up and ready for it."

By this time Will, disturbed by the wind tugging at the canvas top of the wagon, got up and went to the opening at the back of the wagon. "Some rain!" he said to himself, and crawled back into bed.

Now the wind was blowing a gale and the rain coming down in torrents. Joe sprang to his feet and drew on his overalls. The tent was swaying in the wind like a sloop on a stormy sea. The ridgepole of the tent was twisting and squirming like a long, black snake and could be plainly seen with every lurid flash of lightning. The thunder crashed and rolled over the valley, re-echoing against the distant hills. The tent poles swayed like drunken men trying to walk across a slippery deck. Joe grasped one of the poles to keep the tent from going over.

By this time the children were awake. Clara ran to the front upright tent pole and tried to hold it steady, while Lizzie, gathering the three little children together as a hen gathers her chicks together in time of danger. She took them to a bed on the floor of the tent and threw a heavy quilt over them, crawling under it after them, all of them shivering in their scanty night clothes.

At that moment the corner tent stake next to the storm gave way and a deluge of cold water swept into the tent. Libby ran to the corner of the tent, caught up the bottom of the canvas and tried to hold it down, but the canvas was wrenched from her grasp and a deluge of water poured in, and in spite of her efforts everything in the tent was soaked through. Not a sound was heard from the children under the quilt but a prolonged "Oh_o_o_o!" from Eddie as the cold water struck him. Lizzie covered them with a wet woolen blanket. There they remained until the storm was over.

The terrific force of the wind backed the covered wagon several yard to the east. By this time, Will was thoroughly awake, and looking out through the opening in the back of the wagon cover, discovered the wagon was within a few feet of the mules which had been torn loose for the night in an improvised corral. The mules were huddled close together, their tails tucked between their legs and their heads down. The wagon, coming to rest against the corral fence, stopped suddenly, nearly throwing Will off his feet. In a jiffy he was out of the wagon and in the tent, holding the front pole to prevent the tent from caving in entirely.

"Crawl under that blanket where the other kids are!" he shouted to Clara, but instead, Clara hung on to the tent pole to help keep the tent from going over.

The storm was of short duration. The rain suddenly ceased falling and the claps of thunder and flashes of lightning grew fainter and farther away as the storm moved swiftly to the east, leaving a well-soaked immigrant family in their tent on the bank of the river.

Next morning everything in the tent had to be taken out and dried. Joe made racks from a few pieces of lumber that had accumulated about the place and the bedding was laid on them to dry. Every stitch of clothing that was in the tent had to be hung out on the clothes line. It took all the next day to put things to rights so that the family could sleep in dry beds that night. Nothing in the covered wagon was damaged and the mules were none the worse for the storm.

Chapter 4

Building Our Sod House

The corners had been located and Joe had stepped off the lines of the quarter section that had the heaviest grass and the fewest drifts of sand. He and Libby had gone over the tract together to find the most desirable building spot. It was all level so there was so much choice of locations. Finally, it was decided to build near the north line, the nearest point to the river.

"We can drive the stock down there for water if it's necessary," said Joe.

The next day Joe and Libby drove to Sidney, the county seat of Cheyenne County in Nebraska. The papers were made out and signed by a notary.

"That part of the country is known as the Weir valley," the notary told them. "It was named for a widow who came there years ago and took up some land. She couldn't make a go of it and soon moved out. The Indians were still out there and they were not too friendly to white settlers, but the Indians were moved to a reservation only last year. You're just lucky to have come here after they were gone."

After the papers were signed Joe and Libby hurried about their shopping. Supplies for the summer were laid in and machinery was bought for harvesting the hay. Gingham was selected for new dresses for the girls as well as for Libby and new clothing was purchased for the other children.

"It will have to be a sod house," said Joe. "It is the only kind of a house we could build here. It's too far to haul lumber from Sidney and there's not enough timber in these hills to get logs for a log house."

"There's one thing nice about a sod house," said Libby, trying to find something nice to say about a sod house. "It will be cool in summer and warm in winter."

"It certainly will," agreed Joe. "We'll begin building it tomorrow."

"This is pre-emption," he explained to Will, as they prepared to begin building the new house. "The place in Kansas was a homestead. I still have my timber claim right and my soldiers' right. I want to tile on a timber claim as soon as we get this building done, but there's no hurry about that. We couldn't set out trees now, anyway. We can do that early in the spring."

With the new scythe Joe mowed a swath of the luscious grass where the house was to stand. The children frolicked in the new mown hay. What a treat! It reminded them of their home in Kansas when in early summer their father began mowing the hay crop.

The long, straight furrows turned over in the sunlight, glistening like great, black snakes. The grass roots formed a tough fiber in the sod, making it adhesive and easy to handle. He plowed lengthwise of the plot he had chosen and the tough sod was turned up to the sun for the first time in its history. There it had lain for a thousand years waiting for Joe to come and turn it over.

Will followed the plow, cutting the long strips of earth into two foot lengths with a sharp spade. He and his mother loaded them into the wagon and hauled them to where the house was to stand. It was hard work. Lizzie and Clara tugged at the heavy pieces of sod until they managed to drag some of them to the wagon where Will lifted them into the box, being careful not to break them.

The walls of the sod house were soon standing eight feet high. Openings were left at the ends for the windows which Joe had bought in Sidney. A place for a door was left near the west end of the south wall. A deep frame was made and placed in it and rough lumber was sawed and a door made of it. Joe and Will peeled the bark from a pine log the length of the house and with the help of the family managed to hoist it to the top of the low gables for a ridgepole.

"That don't look safe to me!" said Libby. "There's a big knot almost in the middle of the pole. I'm afraid it will break when snow comes in the winter."

"I don't think you need to worry about that," said Joe. "These pine logs are as tough as hickory. They'll stand up under a lot of weight. Besides, that knot is pretty well toward the end of the log and won't get the full weight of the roof."

"I hope you're right, Joe," said Libby, "but I'll always keep an eye on that knot."

"I'll get a post and have it ready in case it threatens to break," he told her teasingly.

Heading for Oregon

Pine poles were brought from the hills and used as rafters and pine boughs were placed over them. On top of the boughs sods were laid carefully to make the roof water tight. During the summer grass grew above the sod, making a small hayfield on the roof.

The fireplace was the family's pride. Built of stones that Joe and Will had quarried from the hills south of the valley and hauled over a rough road that was little better than a cattle trail, it was a possession to be prized. It was built for durability, if not for beauty. For days and nights on end Joe had kept constant vigil at his miniature lime kiln in those same hills where he had prepared enough lime for mortar to build the fireplace and chimney. The sheet iron cook stove stood at one side of the fireplace with the stovepipe extending through a hole in the side of the chimney. A small shelf supported by wooden brackets was placed on the opposite side of the chimney. On this was placed the only books the family possessed: a well worn *Bible*, a dog eared copy of the report of the famous explorers, *Lewis and Clark*, which Joe had almost memorized and *Dr. Gunn's 'Household Remedies'*, which Libby used in every case of illness in the family.

The folding table was covered with oilcloth, which Libby had bought in Sidney, and stood at the end of the room. A few rough benches and camp stools furnished seats for everyone. Three home made bedsteads were placed against three of the walls; one for Libby and Joe, with a trundle bed under it that could be pulled out at night for Hattie and Eddie to sleep in, one for Will at the opposite end of the room, and one, the largest of all, for the three little girls, Lizzie, Clara, and Stella.

"What'll we do for water, Pa?" asked Lizzie anxiously. "We can't carry water from the river in the winter when it's covered with ice."

"Don't worry about that," said her father. "We'll see about the well tomorrow."

Early the next morning as Libby and the girls were getting breakfast they looked out and saw Joe with a willow stick in his hands. He was holding it out in front of him with the pointed end up.

"What are you doing with them two switches, Pa?" asked Stella, running out to where he was. "I'd think one switch would be enough at a time."

But Joe did not answer her. He was giving all of his attention to the willow stick. Within a few minutes the stick seemed to turn in his hands of its own accord and pointed the end downward.

"There's where we'll dig," he said to himself.

"Any luck, Joe?" asked Libby as he sat down to breakfast.

"I got a nibble," replied Joe, "and maybe a real bite."

"Wouldn't it be fine if we found water right here in the door yard?" said Libby. "No more carrying water for washing or anything else. I'd certainly like that!"

"There's water there," said Joe. "It sounds like an old fogy's idea, but just the same it works."

"Let's hope that it works this time," said Libby.

That day Joe and Will took turns digging and before night fall they struck water. The next morning there was a goodly supply of it, but it was blackish and tasted like alkali. They boiled out the water and started digging again. At twenty feet they struck another vein. This time the water was clear and free from alkali.

"That's better," said Joe. "By morning it'll be as clear as crystal."

He was not mistaken. There was not a finer flow of water to be found anywhere.

"The old witch did know where to find water, didn't she, Pa?" said Stella.

"We've just got to have a cow," said Libby. "These children must have milk."

"I'll go to Cedar Creek ranch next week and see if I can by one," replied Joe.

As Joe drove the mule team hitched to the heavy wagon up to the log ranch house a wirey looking man rode up on a buckskin pony. Joe took him to be about thirty five years of age. He swung lightly to the ground, threw the bridle-reins over the pony's head and came to greet Joe.

"Howdy, stranger!" said the man in the dust, brown suit. "What can I do for you this morning?" he said. The two men seated themselves on a wooden bench that stood by the door of the log house, in the shade of a huge willow tree.

"This shade looks good to me," answered Joe. "There's not much of it to be found in this part of the country these days."

"It sure is mighty fine this time of year," said the man. "We wouldn't have this tree if it hadn't been for the crick that runs through the place."

"What's the chance of buying a cow?" Joe asked abruptly. "I'm the fellow that moved into the valley about five miles below here last spring. We've got a bunch of youngsters that have to have milk. Thought you might have a cow for sale. My name's Kirkpatrick," he added, introducing himself.

"Glad to meet you," said the rider. "My name's Mac Radcliffe." The two men shook hands.

"We'll go out an' look 'em over. Ther's plenty of cows to choose from. The milk cows are in that pasture south of the house." Mac removed the bridle from the pony's head and turned him loose. They crossed the creek to a small enclosure where a mixed herd of Holsteins, Durham and Herefords fed quietly on the sloping hillside, cropping the tender, green grass. Nearer the log stable a group of well fed calves frolicked in another, but smaller enclosure.

"Here they are," said Mac. "Take your choice. We don't do much milkin' around here. We let the calves take the milk."

"All good stock," thought Joe. He selected a large, red cow. "Durham's good stock," he said. "Good for both milk and beef."

"She's got a young heifer calf that's not been weaned," said Mac. "That's for sale, too. If you don't want it we'll make veal out of it. We can feed it for awhile."

Joe bought both the cow and the calf. "That'll be a start for the herd we hope to have some day," he said.

Mac deftly cut the cow from the rest of the herd and drove her to a small corral. He then separated the calf from the others and drove it to the same corral. It lost no time in helping itself to the rich milk in its mother's udders, while the two men walked back to the shade of the willow tree by the house.

"Sit down," invited Mac. "It's mighty hot travelin' around this country at this time of year."

"'We don't like to see this country settlin' up," he said frankly, "but, after all, the settlers have as good a right here as the ranchers have. We'll have to fence our pastures now and that'll take a lot of money, but we can take it on the chin with the rest of 'em. The settlers have their troubles, too. If there's anything we can do for you we'll be glad to do it."

Mac Radcliffe meant what he said, as everyone who knew him, could testify. A man of small means he had come west and taken up land and bought other lands. His cattle roamed the hills and valley for miles around. Whether it was on the home ranch or on the public domain mattered not at all to the cattle or to their owner. Pastures were free for the taking, he told Joe. A crew of men helped to look after the cattle. Wolves were plentiful and frequently a cow's carcass was found among the sand hills with the bones gnawed clean. A bear or a mountain lion or a panther found its way to the pastures sometimes and played havoc with the young stock. Rangers made the rounds every day, rain or shine, to see that the cattle were safe and in good condition.

"I hear you have a big roundup in this part of the country every year," said Joe. "It must be a big affair."

"Yes," said Radcliffe. "The whole country is divided into districts and each district has a foreman. I happen to be foreman of this district. There are hundreds of men in the yearly roundups."

"How much territory does a district cover?" asked Joe.

"This one starts just west of North Platte city near the junction of the North and South Platte rivers. That's about a hundred miles east of here and extends to Rush Creek west of here. We work between the North and South forks of the Platte as far as Ogallala. There the crew is divided and part of it goes up the North Platte to the mouth of Rush Creek, then back to Julesburg. The other goes up the South Platte to Julesburg. There the two crews meet and go to the head of Rush Creek and down to its mouth and the round up is over."

"Some job!" said Joe.

Joe hitched the cow to the back of the wagon and by means of a small chute, used for that purpose, the calf was loaded into the wagon.

"Goody! Now we can have all the milk we want," said Hattie.

"Step right up and have a drink, gentlemen!" invited Joe as a group of gaily dressed cowboys came riding across the level valley from the Old Oregon Trail and drew rein at the newly dug well. "It's the finest water you ever tasted; beats booze all hollow."

"Except in case of rattlesnake bite," said Ben Malone, a short, dark fellow who acted as spokesman for the crowd. "Mr. Atkins here," he continued, pointing to a tall, blonde man on a sorrel horse, "keeps a bottle of whiskey at the bottom of the spring at the ranch. He takes a swig of it now and then to keep the varmints from biting him." A chuckle from the rest of the crowd showed their appreciation for Ben's joke.

"It works, too," conceded Mr. Joe Atkins. "I've never had one of them critters bite me yet."

Ben introduced his other two companions: Will Moore and Willis Court, then he stepped to the well curb and took down the tin dipper from its peg. "Does it have a stick in it?" he bantered.

"Yes," piped up Clara. "Eddie put a stick in it yesterday."

Joe looked at Clara in surprise, but said nothing. The cowboys burst into a roar of laughter.

"You're all right!" said Ben. "No doubt Eddie did put a stick in it. That's why the water's so good."

The dipper went the rounds and the cowboys, warm from their ride in the hot sun, drank with relish, then rode away with jingling spurs and creaking chaps, their sombreros shading their eyes from the glaring sun. They rode up the valley toward Cedar Creek ranch, their khaki suits almost invisible against the tawny color of the sand hills.

"They're just like other human beings," said Libby as the men disappeared over the hills. "We've heard so much about the 'wild cowboys' in this part of the country, but I don't believe they're any worse than any other bunch of boys. Did you notice they were all dressed alike except their bandanas were of different colors?"

"That's so they can tell each other apart," said Lizzie.

Clara Kirkpatrick Lau

    By mid summer, half a dozen families or more had taken up claims in the Weir Valley. The Batemans were the first to come. Their claim cornered with the Kirkpatrick's on the southeast. There were six in their family; Mr. and Mrs. Bateman, Susie, and adopted daughter, Maggie, a slip of a girl in her teens, and two boys; Wesley and Huey. To the northwest, John and Andrew Carlson had each homesteaded a quarter section; Andrew's place lying west of John's. John was a married man, but Andrew was single. Mr. Hilgerson and his wife were already building their sod house north of Andrew's place. Mel James' place cornered Joe's to the southwest and just west of them a family by the name of Dixon filed on a claim and built a sod house. There were three in this family: Mr. and Mrs. Dixon and a daughter named Emma. A short time after they came to the community they opened a post office in their home. Willis Court filed on a quarter section of land a mile east of the Kirkpatrick's homestead. A family by the name of Norman settled just east of Bateman's. Berta, a girl of about fourteen, was their only child. Ersel Schmidt, known as the Austrian, or as Schmitty, filed on a claim north of the Kirkpatrick's homestead. Erick Leif and Nels Anderson filed on a claim nearer the river.

    It was a busy summer in the Weir Valley. New sod houses sprang up like mushrooms. Sod stables were being prepared for the ripening hay crop and small herds of cattle and sheep could be seen on every quarter section.

Chapter 5

Fire!

As soon as hay harvest was over, Will had gone to work on the Tom Wagoner ranch on the other side of the river. Money was scarce and the hay crop had not yet been sold.

The two long ricks of grama grass had been capped by noon. They symbolized food and clothing for the immigrant family for the coming year. The haymow of the sod stable was filled to capacity, furnishing feed for a short time for the mules and cow.

The night before, the big hayrack had been filled and the pitchfork thrust into the top of the load at a jaunty angle, and the next morning Joe was ready to take his first load of hay to market. He would go to Sidney this time. It was five miles farther than Lodgpole, but it was a larger town and furnished a better market for farm produce.

The sun was just peeping over the horizon. Libby stood by the load of hay as Joe set off. She waved goodbye as he release the lines from the standard at the corner of the rack and the mules tugged at the heavy load.

"Goodbye!" he called over his shoulder. "Be seeing you day after tomorrow." He pulled up the team to say for the thousandth time, "Be careful of the fire. We don't want to lose any of that precious hay."

"Don't worry," Libby answered. "We will be careful!"

For a moment Libby stood as in a dream. Three days in this distant valley, yet not alone, for there were the children: Will working at the Wagoner ranch, and Joe gone to town. What could they do if a fire should be started either on their own place or on one of the other settlers? She shuddered to think of it. The three days before Joe's return seemed interminable as she looked forward to them.

They had not wakened the children before Joe left that morning, but Lizzie and Clara were up and dressed when Libby re-entered the house. Stella was up, but the two younger children were still in bed. Libby had eaten breakfast with Joe, so the three girls ate their breakfast together.

"Clara and Stella, you wash the dishes while I milk the cow and feed the chickens," said Libby. "Lizzie, do you think you could carry the little sheet-iron stove out and empty the ashes? I noticed last night the ash box was nearly full. I got breakfast by the fireplace this morning, so there surely can't be any fire in the stove. It isn't very heavy, you know."

"Sure! I can carry it out," said Lizzie, and taking down the light stovepipe from the hole in the fireplace chimney the twelve year old girl lifted the little stove and carried it to what seemed to a perfectly bare spot in the dooryard. She emptied the ashes in a neat little pile as she had seen her mother do.

Lizzie was carrying the stove back into the house when a slight crackling sound attracted her attention. She turned quickly and was shocked to see a thin line of smoke rising from a few small straws that lay beside the ashes. Seized with a sudden terror, she hurried back and raked the smoldering heap of ashes with a stick she had been using to remove them from the stove, scattering the fire in every direction.

Instantly the flames formed a circle around the pile of ashes. A sudden breeze caught the burning straws and carried them straight to the long ricks of hay less than a hundred yards distant in a fiery path no wider than Lizzie could have reached with her two small arms.

A scream from Lizzie brought the two girls from the house, and Libby, leaving the cow unmilked, ran to the stable door.

"Water, bring water quickly!" she shouted.

Clara and Stella grabbed a large water bucket and ran to the pump.

"Hurry, it will burn the hay!" called Libby as she turned and ran back into the stable for some gunny sacks.

Lizzie, now somewhat recovered from her first shock, snatched one of the sacks from her mother's hands and began fighting the fire. Clara picked up the milk pail which her mother had brought from the stable and ran back to the well. Stella took another gunny sack and whipped the smoldering tufts of grass along the path.

But their efforts were in vain. The breeze had carried the flames straight to the haystacks. Nothing short of a miracle could stop them now; but no miracle happened. Glowing darts of fire shot upward and onward like little demons running a race to see which could reach the haystacks first. With a sudden flare a tiny flame won the race. It leaped to the side of the nearest stack and climbed quickly to the top. Snatching at the loose stems in its glee it shot sparks and darts of flame upward in a red spiral that seemed to reach the sky.

Lizzie's scream and Libby's shout attracted the attention of their two Swedish neighbors who were working in their own hayfield to the north.

"Vat's all the fuss about?" queried John, the elder brother.

"I see smoke!" replied Andrew. "Look! Look!" he shouted. "Joe's haystacks are afire!"

The two men quickly unhitched their team and each, mounting a horse, came at full gallop to the scene of the fire.

"Hitch de horses to Joe's plow!" shouted John. "Andy, you plow fireguards between this place an' ourn and I'll help here!"

With quick, efficient hands the two men hitched the horses to Joe's breaking plow and Andy was soon plowing fireguards the full length of the line that separated the two claims. John, with a gunny sack in one hand and a bucket of water in the other fought back the flames as they spread along the path to the stable. Libby struck at the fiery demons wherever they showed their fiendish heads near the house. There was nothing that could save the hay now. Fortunately the house and stable were made of sod and would not burn, but there were the mower and rake and other valuable articles standing about the place that must be saved if possible.

Suddenly the wind veered to the west and the path of the flames was turned eastward. The Carlson place was safe, at least for the present.

John came to the well for water.

"Is Willis Court at home?" asked Libby, who had pumped water most of the time since the fire had started.

"No, he vork by Cedar Creek ranch," replied John.

"Then, there's no one at his house," said Libby, "and the Bateman's house is in danger, too. I see Mr. Bateman plowing a fireguard this side of their houses. If only there was another plow down there they might stop the fire from going any farther."

By this time Andy had completed his task of plowing and, mounting one of his big, brown horses and leading the other, hurried to the house. "If someone could tek our horses over to Bateman's," he said, wiping the perspiration from his ruddy face, "Ves, one could take one of their plows an' go down an' help his fadder. It'd double the number of furrows dis side of dem houses. Dat ought to stop it." He paused for breath and continued, turning to Libby, "Can't your two oldest girls' tek de horses to Bateman's house?" he asked. "Dat'll leave John an' me to help with the fire here an' at our house."

Libby's heart sank. She was on the point of refusing to allow her two little girls to undertake so dangerous a journey.

"Let us go, Ma! Please let us go!" pleaded Clara.

"Sure, we can go!" echoed Lizzie. "I started the fire and I want to do all I can to stop it."

And so it was decided. The two girls mounted the great farm horses with their jingling harness still on them. Without looking back they urged the horses forward while Libby prayed they reach their destination in safety.

It was a mile to the Bateman's place, but the two horses, bearing their precious burdens, lost no time.

"What's this for?" asked Mrs. Bateman as the two girls clambered down from the backs of the horses.

"They said," panted Lizzie, "They said – for Wes – to – take the horse an' plow fireguards – on this side of Willis Court's house."

The fireguards were plowed. As evening approached the wind died down and the fire seemed to slacken its speed towards the east. Soft dews lulled the demons to sleep, and all that was left of the conflagration were a few spots of flame that darted up for a moment. These were laid to rest forcibly by the deft wielding of a wet gunny sack in the hands of a sturdy settler. A pall of smoke hung over the valley, and an occasional tongue of flame thrust its darts skyward.

It was a subdued and stricken family that sat down to their evening meal long after supper time. With blackened hands and faces hastily washed at the tub of water by the pump that sat at the table. The tears streaming down their faces left white streaks on their pale cheeks. The weary mother tried to comfort her children as she coaxed them to eat their frugal meal; but the strain of the day had been too much for them.

Lizzie laid her head on her arms on the table and burst into tears. "It's all my fault!" she sobbed. "What'll

Heading for Oregon

Pa say when he comes home and finds everything burnt up?"

"It ain't your fault!" comforted Clara, putting her arm caressingly around Lizzie's shoulders. "Any of us probably would've done the same thing. You couldn't help it, so don't cry, Lizzie. Please don't cry!" and Clara leaned her head against the table and sobbed.

The three younger children burst into tears and Libby carried them off to bed and tucked them in gently, humming a lullaby to quiet them.

The supper dishes were left on the table that night. Everyone was too tired to care whether they were washed or not. Eddie tossed in his sleep and muttered, "Pump more water! Figntin'fire!"

Lizzie lay with wide eyes staring into space, reliving the harrowing experiences of the day; carrying water, fighting fire with a gunny sack, riding the long mile to the Bateman's place. Libby put the untouched food into the wooden cupboard, tiptoed to the bed where her two older girls lay and listened for a moment. Clara was fast asleep, but Lizzie lay staring into the darkness. The mother knew that her child was broken hearted and needed comforting.

"Darling," she said, "I want you to know that no one blames you for starting the fire. It was merely an accident that might have happened to any of us."

Lizzie pressed her mother's hand. It was comforting just to have her near.

"We are all well and able to work and we'll make a living somehow," continued Libby. "And remember, dear, God will care for his children. Now go to sleep.

You and all of us need rest. Good night, sleep tight and wake up bright in the morning light."

On Libby the strain of the day had been terrific. The crop of hay and even the stubble from which the cow and chickens could at least have gleaned part of their food lay in ashes across the broad meadows. Not even a grasshopper upon which the chickens thrived remained. The hardships that loomed before her were appalling. How could she ever meet Joe when he returned home and see his look of distress as he learned of their loss?

She stood in the doorway of the sod house, gazing out into the night. A limitless dome of sky, with some clouds drifting lazily to the east, looked down on the valley. Every moment the darkness was closing in as though the night were stealing, unperceived, across the darkened valley, and she alone could see it coming. "Let it come!" thought Libby. "It can't make matters any worse than they are!" O, God, how weary she was! At last she lay in bed, staring into the darkness. In fitful sleep she started, rose and hurried to the window, thinking she hear fire crackling, but the world was dark and still.

It was late when Joe returned to his humble home two days after the fire. Libby had watched for the wagon to come over the sand hills and wind down the rocky road to the valley. She strained her eyes in the twilight until it was too dark to see, then sat waiting for him by the open door after the children had gone to bed. She heard the heavy wagon rumbling long before it reached the stable, waiting for him at the gate with a lantern in her hand. The tear stains were gone from her pale cheeks and a resolute look was in her dark eyes.

"How did it happen, Libby?" he asked after he had greeted her. "I smelled the smoke before I reached the valley. Then when I came nearer the stable I could see by the light of the lantern that everything about the place was black."

Libby told the whole sickening story. "Poor Lizzie is heartbroken," she continued. "She thinks it's all her fault, but anyone might have done the same thing. I thought the fire in the stove was out. There hadn't been any fire in it since the day before she took the stove out to empty the ashes. It's worse than you think, Joe," she said, trying to prepare him for the shock that awaited him the next morning when he could see the ravages of the conflagration. "The haystacks are completely destroyed, except for the hay in the stable, there's not a straw on the place."

"It's a hard road to travel," replied Joe, "but we've traveled hard roads before and I guess we can do it again. The Lord will provide."

"Yes, that's our only hope," sobbed Libby, turning away to hide her tears.

The next morning Joe began his summer plowing, "There's no use crying over spilled milk," he said. He plowed long, even furrows across the timber claim next to the house. His ruddy face streaked with the blackened dust. The summer rains, if there happened to be any and the winter's snows would mellow the soil so that trees could be planted there in the spring.

"Hay, Hay! Look, Pa, look! The hay didn't all burn," called Hattie, as a steak of blue calico shot across the burned grass to the end of the furrow where Joe had stopped the mules to give them a breathing spell.

Joe looked in the direction in which Hattie pointed. Sure enough a huge load of hay was making its way towards the Mel James corner. Joe watched it coming. It turned north on the cross road that had been laid out along the section line, and slowly winded its way toward him the big hayrack creaking as it lumbered nearer, the wheels making a grinding sound as they plowed through the loose soil. He lifted the child to the cross-bar of the plow and held her there, waiting. The driver stopped his team a few yards from them and a voice called from the front of the load, "Hello there! Thought you might find use for some hay for the mules and cow. Mac Radcliffe sent me down with this load."

"Sure, I can use a load of hay," replied Joe. "It was fine of Mac to think of it. We'll unload it right over there by the stable. I'll be there pronto."

The hay was soon unloaded and piled in a neat stack. "How much did Mac say it was worth?" asked Joe.

"He didn't say nothin' about the price," said Will Moore. "He just told me to bring it over. He's not the kind of person to charge a neighbor anything when he's in trouble. Forget it! We all have our ups and downs, an' this is the time you're havin' you downs."

Joe's voice was husky as he thanked him for the hay as he mounted the wagon and drove away.

"Talk about the Godless cowboys!" he said to Libby as he sat at the dinner table. "There's not a finer bunch of men in the world than them cowboys."

That afternoon a light wagon drew up at the door of the sod house. Libby recognized the driver. It was Ben Malone, the cowboy who had introduced his companions at the well a few days before.

"We butchered a cow this morning" he drawled, "an' thought you all might be able to use part of it."

"We certainly can!" replied Libby, "but we want to pay you for this. Will Moore wouldn't take anything for the hay, but we must pay for this meat. This is a real godsend and don't know what we'd done without it."

But Ben would not listen. "That's all right," he said. "If you can use it that's all there is to it."

The next morning a sack of flour was leaning against the door as Joe opened it to go to the stable to hitch the mules to the plow.

"I'll bet the Carlsons brought that," he said. "They're as good as gold. How they must have worked to keep that fire from taking everything in the valley!"

Day after day for more than a week the food kept coming in: coffee and tea, sugar and pails of milk. It was amazing, the amount of food that could be stored in the neighboring sod houses, yet there it was groceries and meat enough to last the stricken family until they could get on their feet again.

Will came home from the Wagoner ranch from across the river as soon as he could after he heard about the fire. It was lucky for the family that he had a job. "Here's an extra ten you can take to the old man," said Tom Wagoner as he paid Will for the last month's work. "Looks like them settlers is havin' their troubles."

Chapter 6

Thanksgiving Turkey

The crisp, cold air made the men shiver as they quit work for the night. Andy Johnson's place was on the Divide which stretched in an apparently endless, undulating plain from the tops of the sand hills where the desert began to the southward, sloping to the South Platte River. Joe had helped Andy with his fall plowing on his desert ranch and, that being finished, Joe was ready to leave for home.

"What'll you take for one of them turkeys?" asked Joe as Andy paid him for his work.

"O, I don' no jist what they're sellin' for," replied Andy. "Whatever you think they're worth."

Joe offered him what he considered a fair price and the largest turkey of the flock was sold. Andy didn't sell his turkeys by the pound, but by the head.

"We'll ketch that one in the mornin' before they go out to the range," said Andy.

"Them turks make their own livin' mostly on grasshoppers an' whatever grain they git pickin' around the stubble, which ain't much, but they seem to keep fat in spite of poor pickin'."

The next morning Joe and Andy went out to the turkey lot which was enclosed in a tight picket fence. "That's to keep the coyotes from getting' at 'em," remarked Andy.

Heading for Oregon

The large, fat gobbler was herded into a corner of the yard and captured and put into a wooden crate, ready for Joe to take when he went home.

By noon the heavy lumber wagon was jolting along over the dusty road through the sage brush country, then down over the sand hills to the valley below, arriving at Joe's home shortly before dark. The heavy crate was lifted from the wagon and place on the ground by the chicken yard gate. The bewildered bird, jolted by the constant motion of the wagon, staggered and almost fell as Joe set it on its feet in the chicken yard. Joe then unhitched the mules and led them to the stable.

Libby had just finished milking the cow and came, pail in hand, to see the addition to their poultry flock. The children gathered about the enclosure, hanging onto the picket fence. Libby set the pail of milk in the wagon box and picked up a pan of wheat which she had brought for the chickens, and scattered it on the ground for them. Chickens came flying from every direction to get the feed, but the turkey, still dazed, stood looking about him. Clara climbed to the top of the gate post to get a better view of the new comer.

"Where did you get him, Pa?" she asked. "Are we going to keep him?"

"Sure, we're going to keep him," replied Joe, "for awhile, at least," he added.

The big red rooster, Samson, cock of the flock, inspected the newcomer critically for a moment, and then sided up to him, shaking a threatening spur. The turkey, too confused to defend himself, walked slowly to the farther corner of the pen, eyeing his adversary contemptuously.

"O, look!" shouted Clara, "Samson'll kill him! Take him out, Pa! Take him out!"

"I guess he'll be all right," answered her father. "If he can't take care of himself he's not much good," and went on about his work.

The red rooster made another pass at the turkey. This time the turkey walked away from him and began eating with the chickens. A third time Samson attacked him. That was the limit! The turkey reached out a long neck and gave his tormentor a sharp pinch on his red gills. The rooster looked surprised and went quietly to the opposite side of the pen.

"It looks a lot like snow," said Joe, as he and Libby walked towards the house. "See that bank of black clouds in the northwest? It'll storm before morning."

Libby glanced up in the direction in which Joe pointed. "Yes," she said, "its cold enough."

They reached the house and Joe hung his slicker coat on the peg behind the door, and then went to the fireplace where a bright fire was burning and held his benumbed fingers to the cheery flame. "The fire feels good even if it is only November," he said.

Libby strained the milk into a large tin pan which she set on the shelf in the wooden cupboard, then busied herself about the evening meal.

Clara sat on the gate post long after the chickens had gone to roost. The turkey, not knowing where to go, sat down in a corner of the pen and Clara left him there for the night. She went into the house and threw her coat onto the bed and lay down, resting her head on the coat.

"Don't you feel well, Clara?" asked her mother anxiously. This was an unusual performance for the husky eleven year old Clara.

"Yes, I'm all right," answered Clara. "I was just thingkin' about that mean old rooster fightin' the new turkey." She lay on the bed for a few minutes, then got up and went to the fire.

"How's my tow headed girl this evening?" asked Joe, as Clara seated herself on a low stool by the fire.

"O, I'm fine," replied Clara, "but I'm afraid Samson'll kill the new turkey by morning when it's light enough to see."

"He's able to take care of himself," said her father, as he picked up an old newspaper that lay on the floor and sat down to read it. "What do you think would be a good name for the turkey?" he asked.

"I think we'll call him Daniel," said Clara. "He's almost in a lion's den. Old Samson may kill him in the morning. Do you think he'll kill him, Pa?"

"I wouldn't be surprise," answered her father, teasingly.

"Don't tell her that or she'll be out there before breakfast to see if he's still alive," said Libby.

"O, he'll be all right. Don't worry about the turkey," said Joe.

Clara was far from being satisfied. She went out again late in the evening to see how the newcomer fared, but found him still sitting in the corner of the chicken pen.

By morning a foot of snow lay over the valley and the thermometer stood far below the freezing point. The wind whistled around the corners of the sod house and a gust of icy wind roared into the room as Joe opened the door. It made the fire he had just kindled flicker and nearly go out. It carried with it great sheets of snow that twisted and writhed in the blast like shredded lengths of cotton batting hanging in the wind. Joe drew his heavy coat about him and buttoned it close about his throat, then pulled his woolen cap down over his ears. He shoveled a path to the stable, did the usual chores and then hurried back to the house.

After breakfast Libby took her darning basket and sat down in her favorite chair by the fireplace. The fire was inviting on a morning like this. Joe was mending his boots as the children were playing about the big, dark room, all but Clara. She took in the situation at one furtive glance. Now was her chance! She walked quietly to where the wraps hung in the corner behind the door, took down her mother's big, brown shawl and wrapped it about her head and shoulders, with only a few wisps of tow colored hair showing about her face. She opened the door a very little crack, just wide enough for her slender body to squeeze through and stepped out into the storm.

The path her father had shoveled was so dim that she could scarcely see it, but she reached the stable without any difficulty. Like a flash she ran toward the poultry enclosure, the shawl blowing wildly about her small figure, the icy wind stinging her cheeks.

Not a chicken was in sight. Clara entered the crude chicken house and looked anxiously about in the dim light, but could see nothing of the turkey. She peered through the murky light and could see the chickens on the roost. Old Samson sat by himself, looking very disconsolate. She could see that his red comb was torn and bleeding and both turkey and chicken feathers were scattered about the hen house. After further search she discovered the big turkey sitting on the highest perch, looking very innocent, but very wise. Clara went over to him and stroked his soft feathers. "He'll be all right after he gets acquainted," she thought.

Seeing that all was well with the turkey she drew the shawl closer about her and stepping out into the storm looked in the direction of the house, but no house loomed before her startled eyes. The path her father had shoveled from the house to the stable could no longer be seen and the wind cut her bare face like a knife.

What should she do? She certainly could not stay there much longer. She would freeze to death! Clara went into the stable where the mules and the cow stood shivering. It was somewhat warmer in there, but she knew she couldn't stay there either. She opened the door a very little crack and the wind caught at her shawl and whipped it about her. She knew where the house was even if she couldn't see it through the blinding snow. She resolved to take a chance. Her father had often told her, "take a chance even if you don't know whether you will win or not." She took the chance!

Out into the storm she ventured, making a bee line, as she thought, for the house. On and on she ran, throwing her weight against the wind. It was hard work plowing through the deep drifts against the terrific gale. She kept looking for the house. Surely she must be nearly there, but still she couldn't see it. Her feet slipped on the frozen snow and she almost fell to the ground, but she righted herself and ran on, gasping for breath in the biting air.

What if she should fall and be buried in the snow! The thought chilled her more than the cold wind did. In a fringy Clara could see her parents out in the storm looking for her, but she would be lying buried under the deep drifts, cold and white, frozen to death! Now she was running against the wind and calling to them to come to her rescue. How tired she felt! She must lie down and rest, but no, that would never do! If she lay down out there she would soon be covered with snow and they wouldn't find her until the snow melted in the spring.

Clara stopped for breath. She couldn't go any farther! "O, God!" she cried in terror. "I'm lost! Please show me the way home!"

As if an answer to her prayer, she turned suddenly and looked back.

A dark mass like a bank of clouds loomed before her frightened eyes. "That's the house!" she cried hysterically and started running toward the dark object.

"If that child's gone to the stable she'll never get back in this storm," said Libby, hastily laying her work aside. "Did any of you see her go out?"

"Gone to the stable!" echoed Joe. "What on earth would she go to the stable for on a morning like this?"

"You know she was worried about that turkey last night," said Libby. "It's very likely she's gone to the stable to see what has happened to it."

Joe was drawing on the boot he had been mending, the wax end still dangling from the patch he was sewing on. He put on his coat and cap and hurried to the door. By this time the whole family was in frenzy, looking in every possible nook and corner for the missing child.

Just as he reached the door, a bedraggled little figure in a big, brown shawl staggered into his arms.

"I just wanted to see if the turkey was still alive," she sobbed, "and I got lost in the storm."

"You mean you wanted to see if Daniel was still alive in the lion's den?" asked her father.

"Yes," she sobbed, "and he's still alive."

"Tomorrow is Thanksgiving Day," said Libby, "but I think we'd better slay Daniel today. We don't want to have any more little girls lost in the snowstorm, looking for a turkey."

Chapter 7

Christmas

In the fall after the fire had swept through the valley, burning their hay, Joe and Libby made their last trip of the season to Sidney, thirty five miles distant, returning home three days later. Supplies for the winter were unloaded and stored in every corner of the sod house. Libby brought in a large cardboard box and set it on the kitchen table.

"What's in that box?" asked Stella, who had a prominent bump of curiosity.

"I bought some yarn for stockings," replied her mother, evading Stella's question. "You know we always need plenty of stocking yarn."

She carried the box to the shelves at the head of her bed and placed it on the dirt floor under the bottom shelf. "It'll be all right there," she said to herself. "Nobody'll bother it, I guess."

Snow flew before Joe got around to hauling his winter's wood. On a day in late November he came home from the hills where he had cut the scrub pine trees, with his wagon piled high with wood – or was it all wood? He stopped at the stable and left part of his load, then brought the remainder and threw it onto the great woodpile near the house. No one seemed to notice the delay.

It was nearing Christmas time and Libby was worried. Money was so scarce! In fact, the family had little ready cash except what Will could spare from the meager wages he was earning at the Wagoner ranch.

"Do you think Santa will come this Christmas?" asked Hattie wistfully, as Libby sat by the fireplace knitting. "I'd like a dolly for Christmas."

Her mother turned her face to the fire, pretending not to hear. She, too, had been thinking the same thing. "We'll see," she said presently. Something must be done! The children must not be allowed to miss their accustomed Christmas treat.

"I want a ball for Christmas," chimed in Eddie. "Santa will bring me a big, red ball. Won't he, Ma?"

"Maybe so," his mother answered.

Just at that moment a man on horseback drew rein at the door of the sod house. "Hello there!" shouted a cheery voice.

Libby lay her knitting in the basket beside her chair and stepped to the door. "Good morning!" she said. "Won't you come in? It's pretty cold outside this morning."

It was Ben Malone of the Cedar Creek ranch. "Some of us is goin' to Sidney in the mornin'," he drawled, "an' we thought you might want to send for something, since it's nearly Christmas."

Libby looked puzzled. Of course she wanted to send for something, but where was the money to come from with which to pay for it?

"Yes, I do want a few things from town," she faltered, and turning to the fireplace, took down a fifty cent piece which she had been saving for weeks.

"It'll at least buy them a little treat," she thought and stepping outside she said to Ben in a low tone, "here's fifty cents. It's all I can spare. I'd be glad if you would bring me some apples and oranges for the children's Christmas."

Ben took the coin and dropped it into his overcoat pocket. "I'll sure do that," he said. "So long!" he called as he rode off toward the ranch.

Night after night Libby sat at the machine and sewed long after the children had gone to bed. There was a bright red calico dress for Stella with its dainty ruffles trimmed with white edging, small aprons for the two older girls and numerous garments for the rest of the family. Joe sat near her mending shoes. It seemed there were always shoes to be mended! The light from their one kerosene lamp shone on the little table between them.

It was the day before Christmas. The snow lay knee deep on the level and the thermometer registered forty below zero, but in spite of the cold, the pioneer family was snug and comfortable in the thick walled sod house with its great fireplace stacked high with pine logs. Libby sat by the fire with Eddie on her lap. Hattie leaned against her mother's knee. "Tell us a story, Ma," she begged.

"What kind of a story, darling?" her mother asked.

"Tell us about the Baby Jesus," suggested Stella, as she seated herself on a small stool beside Libby.

"That is a good Christmas story," said her mother. *"Once upon a time,"* she began, *"there was a tiny baby born in the little town of Bethlehem."*

"Go on, Mama!" coaxed Eddie as Libby paused. Then she told the whole beautiful story of the coming of the Christ Child.

Clara and Lizzie, their half knitted stockings in their hands, came and stood behind their mother. They, too, loved to hear the often told story.

As the story was completed, the sound of sleigh bells rang out on the frosty air. Joe went to the window and looked out. Libby came and looked over his shoulder as the children clustered about them. The sleigh drew up at the deep set doorway and a muffled voice called, "hello there, anybody home?" It was Ben Malone again.

Joe went to the door. "Hello, yourself;" he answered, as a small, dark complexioned man wearing a bearskin coat and cap alighted from the sleigh.

"O, goody, goody!" squealed Hattie. "It's Santa Claus! I knowed he'd come! Goody, goody!" and she danced a merry little jig about the room.

"Did you bring me my ball?" called Eddie, but the little driver did not answer. Instead, he stepped to the back of the sleigh and with Joe's help lifted a large box from its hiding place in the back of the sleigh, then another and another followed until the family stared in open eyed wonder.

"Thanks a lot," said Joe, looking bewildered. "I'll have to ask you to wait awhile for pay for all this, but thanks just the same."

"You don't owe me anything," said Ben. "The fellers at the ranch chipped in to give the kids a little treat for Christmas," he drawled. Then mounting the seat of the sleigh he drew the lines tight and was gone.

And such a treat! The large box was filled with big, red apples. In the other boxes were oranges, nuts, and candies and at the bottom of one box was a side of bacon and other foods. Tears flooded Libby's eyes as she watched the sleigh disappear over the sand hills, and Joe's voice was husky as he said, "the good Lord couldn't have made better neighbors than the men at that ranch."

Supper was over and the younger children fast asleep, dreaming of the fun they would have on Christmas day. Lizzie and Clara were far too excited to sleep. They couldn't have closed their eyes just for a little nap even if they did go to bed. They drew their chairs nearer to the glowing fire where Joe and Libby were sitting. They all found comfort in being close together that cold winter night.

Libby was thinking of the night not so long ago when Joe had left part of his load of "wood" at the stable. As though reading her mind, Joe said to her in a low tone, "now's the time to bring it in."

"Yes, bring it in," replied Libby. The girls looked puzzled. Joe put on his heavy coat and cap and left the room.

"Where's he goin' at this time of night?" asked Lizzie.

"I'll bet he's got a surprise hid outside somewhere," said Clara, but Libby was busy knitting and did not answer.

A few minutes later Joe opened the door and entered, dragging a small pine tree by the trunk, its bushy top scraping on the hard, frozen snow making a squeaking sound.

Heading for Oregon

"Look out, Joe! You'll knock the lamp over!" exclaimed Libby, as she and the two girls sprang to their feet and began tugging at the tree. It was all they could do to get it in through the door, but it was soon inside and Joe was placing it in the center of the room. "I'll get the brace, Will made for it the last time he was at home," he said.

It was a beautiful tree! Such clusters of long needles and symmetrical cones! The trunk was tapering and graceful, and the bark, though it had a few pitch spots on it, was smooth and glossy. The room was filled with its fragrance.

"It's bed time now," said Joe. "Let's leave the rest of it for the big day tomorrow. I'm off for bed."

"Let's trim the tree tonight!" exclaimed Lizzie, "and have it all ready when they wake up in the morning. But what'll we trim it with?"

"I think I can find something to trim it with," said their mother, stepping softly to the head of the bed so as not to disturb Joe who was already snoring. She drew out the big cardboard box, which was supposed by the girls to contain knitting yarn, and placed it on a chair in front of the fire. "We'll find plenty of trimmings in this box," she said, and lifting the lid revealed rolls of colored papers and tinsel. A few colored balls were tucked away in one corner of the box and a package of popcorn was hidden under the tinsel.

"O, goody!" exclaimed Clara. "That's enough to trim two trees."

"I'll be the popper," said Lizzie, and dragging the Dutch oven from its corner by the fireplace raked coals onto the hearth and set the oven on them. She poured corn into the oven and placed the lid over it. Soon they could hear the pop, pop of the kernels under the iron lid. Clara brought an earthen crock to put the snowy kernels in and began stringing them on long, white threads. When enough corn had been popped, Lizzie helped string the kernels. These were draped on the tree. Libby cut long streamers from the colored paper, twisted them slightly and with the tinsel fastened the tips of the branches. Libby fashioned a star from tinfoil from an old tobacco wrapper, and climbing upon a chair, fastened it to the top of the tree.

With their task completed, Libby and her two daughters stepped back to view their handiwork. The gleaming balls and tinsel caught up the beams of light from the glowing fire and reflected them to the dark walls and rugged rafters of the sod house. The star picked up the points of light and carried them to the darkest corners of the room.

They filled the stockings of the three younger children with the goodies brought by Ben Malone, with a big, red apple in the toe of each stocking.

"We don't need to hang up our stockings, do we Clara?" asked Lizzie. Clara made no reply, but smiled a faint acquiescence.

"We'd better leave it now," said Libby. "It will please the children and your father, too, when they see it in the morning."

Christmas day dawned clear and cold. Icicles draped the eaves of the sod house, and Joe stamped the snow from his heavy boots as he came in from feeding the mules and milking the cow.

"Merry Christmas!" greeted him as he entered the door.

"It might be a merry Christmas if it wasn't so cold," he said. "It's as cold as blazes outside."

"Where did you get that tree?" shouted Stella as she danced merrily about the Christmas tree.

"Did Santa bring that, too?" inquired Hattie.

"I'm looking for my big, red ball," exclaimed Eddie, peering under the tree. "Did he bring it?"

"I don't see any ball," said his father. "Maybe we'll find it later."

"Breakfast's ready!" announced Libby, and the happy family sat down to bacon and eggs with hot biscuits as they had not done for many a day.

After breakfast the family gathered about the Christmas tree.

"Let's have a program," said Joe. "This is going to be an impromptu program."

"What's a 'mpomtu pogum?" asked Stella.

"It's a program where everyone says what he happens to think," replied her father.

"Then I'll say what I happen to think right now," said Stella.

"Well, what do you happen to think?" asked Joe.

"Pass the candy!" demanded Stella.

"Say please," teased Clara who happened to be nearest the candy dish that stood on the breakfast table.

"Please, pretty please!" begged Stella. "Ma, make her give me some candy."

"Clara, don't tease," said her mother.

The candy dish went around. "Remember, you kids," warned Clara, "only one piece apiece."

"Well, let's go on with our program," said Joe. "Stella, you may be first."

Surprised, Stella took the candy from her mouth and holding it in sticky fingers, sang in her clear, childish voice:

> P-s-e pass in the wondrous was
> In the shelter of the fold.

It was a song she had made up when a mere baby and she sang it to the tune, *There Were Ninety and Nine*, which she had often heard sung around the family altar.

"That's all right," said Joe, smiling. "The words could be different, but they'll do. Clara, what's on your mind?"

Clara came bravely to her feet and sang,

> I love candy. I love toys
> I love the girls, but I don't love boys.

"How do you know you don't love boys?" bantered Lizzie. "You don't know any boys."

"I do, too!" countered Clara. "I know Wes Bateman, but he's too old for me, an' I know Huey, but he's just a kid."

"Hattie has a little piece to speak," said Libby, and pointing a dimpled finger toward the star at the top of the tree the child recited:

> *Twinkle, twinkle little star,*
> *I know what you are.*

"That's fine," said Joe. "Eddie, do you have a piece to speak?"

"He's too busy with his piece of candy," said Libby. "He'll do his speaking later."

"Now," said Joe, "let's sing our Christmas carols we've been practicing for the last two weeks."

Carols were sung and the rafters of the sod house rang with their echoes, then all listened while Lizzie recited:

> *T'was the night before Christmas*
> *And all through the house*
> *Not a creature was stirring,*
> *Not even a mouse.*

"I hear a mouse!" exclaimed Eddie from his mother's lap, as Lizzie recited:

> *With a jolly old driver*
> *So lively and quick,*
> *I knew in a moment*
> *It must be St. Nick.*

"It's wite by the door! I hear it!" persisted Eddie.

Just at that moment the door of the sod house was thrown wide open and, sure enough, there stood the jolly old saint himself with a long, white beard flowing over his chest, but his coat and cap were plain, heavy woolen garments without the fur trimmings. A look of surprise shone on the children's faces, then a burst of laughter and a clapping of hands greeted him.

"Did you bring my big, red ball?" asked Eddie.

"You bet I did!" answered Santa. "I'll see if I can find it."

"There it is wite on top!" exclaimed Eddie, and sure enough there was a big, red rubber ball in the top of the pack.

Santa tossed the ball and it rolled on the dirt floor. Eddie scrambled from his mother's lap and ran after it.

"Is my dolly there?" asked Hattie timidly.

"I'll see," said Santa, and fumbling through his pack found the doll. It was a large doll with cloth body and bisque head. It was dressed in baby clothes and showed evidence of careful hand stitching where the head was joined to the body.

Hattie cuddled her treasure in her arms.

"What's your dolly's name?" asked Stella.

"Her name is Susie," promptly answered the little mother. "O, my dear, dear dolly! Ain't she sweet, Mama?" she cooed, carrying the doll to her mother.

"Yes, she is sweet, darling," answered her mother, smiling. "I'm glad you like it."

There was a new red dress with white edgings for Stella, small, ruffled aprons for Lizzie and Clara, and warm woolen socks for Joe. Santa handed Joe another pair of socks. "Just hold these for awhile and I'll tell you what to do with them," he said. Joe looked at Santa with reigned surprise, but said nothing.

"Here's the biggest parcel of all," said Santa, reaching to the bottom of the sack. "The tag says, to the best wife and mother in the world. I wonder who that could be," he mused. "O, I know! She's sitting right there by the table," and he tossed the bundle to Libby.

"Thank you, Santa!" she said, as she unfolded an ample length of worsted goods, enough for a dress for herself.

"Now, let's see what's on this nice tree," said Santa. "Here's a stocking full of goodies for Eddie and one for Hattie, yes, and one for Stella."

The stockings were quickly distributed and Santa, stepping to the door, turned and bowed. "I wish you all a merry Christmas!" he exclaimed and disappeared, closing the door behind him.

The children rushed to the window, hoping to see him and his sleigh dashing down the snowy road, but they could see nothing but a bare waste of drifted snow.

Soon there was a knocking at the door. "I wonder who that could be!" said Libby. She stepped to the door and opened it.

"Merry Christmas," called a clear young voice. "What are the chances of getting a handout? I'm hungry!"

Libby threw her arms about her tall young son and drew him into the sod house, and exclaimed, "Dinner will be ready before you know it."

Everyone but Joe and Libby looked surprised, for they thought that Will was still working across the river for Tom Wagoner.

Such a dinner! Roast beef, potatoes and brown gravy and everything that goes to make up a good

Clara Kirkpatrick Lau

Christmas dinner, thanks to the cowboys of Cedar Creek ranch.

"Let's sing, *Joy to the World*, said Joe, and the rafters of the sod house echoed to the melody of the grand old carol.

Chapter 8

The Ridgepole in the Sod House

When the sod house was built the summer before, Libby had protested against the men putting up that ridgepole. There was a great knot almost in the middle of it. "It's not safe!" she declared. "It may be all right this summer, but when the snow comes in the winter, look out! It will make the roof so heavy there's danger of its breaking down," and she visualized the interior of their new home with its seven occupants, five of them children under twelve years of age, if that pole should give way. She shuddered to think of the consequences.

"I know it's not safe," Joe admitted, "but it's the only straight tree we could find that was long enough. It was that or nothing."

"It had better be nothing than run the risk of having the roof cave in on us some winter night," countered Libby, her pale face flushing. She was usually even-tempered, but sometimes things got on her nerves.

"I'll get a post to set under it the next time I go to the woods," Joe said, biting his lip half angrily.

Joe had kept his promise. The post had been prepared and laid by the side of the house near the door so that it would be handy when he found time to put it up. He had sawed a two-by-six scantling to the proper length and placed it beside the post.

The fall work had kept him busy, and he had almost forgotten it was there. Anyway, the ridgepole seemed to be holding, and he had not worried about it.

It was after Christmas now, and snow had been falling intermittently for weeks and lay three feet on the level. It was not quite so deep on the roof. The warmth from the fireplace and the cook stove had melted it somewhat, but that had only made it more compact as the moisture had seeped through the sod and soaked the pine poles that supported the roof.

"Don't you think we'd better put that post under the knot in that ridgepole?" Libby asked anxiously one evening. "The snow's getting pretty deep up there."

"Yes, I'll see to that tomorrow," Joe replied, thrusting his awl through the leather of the boot he was mending. He drew the wax-end through and fastened the thread. "I must do that tomorrow. It's too late to start a job like that today."

"Better do it today," said Libby. "Tomorrow may be too late."

She laid down the stocking she was darning and put the mending basket on the shelf at the foot of the bed. "How short the days are getting!" she said. "It's nearly dark and only four o'clock." "Clara," she added, "will you stir up the fire in the fireplace? I'll make some biscuits for supper."

"And are you going to bake them in the Dutch oven?" inquired Clara.

"Yes!" said her mother. "That's what I was thinking of doing."

Soon after supper the children tumbled into bed. These long nights were a good time to go to bed early and sleep late.

Joe and Libby sat awhile after the children had gone to bed, Joe smoking his corncob pipe and reading *Jane' almanac*, while Libby sat combing her long auburn hair. She braided it in two shining braids as sparks of light danced in and out of the glowing mass. It was good to rest awhile after the noise and toil of the day.

Joe finished his pipe and knocked the ashes out against the side of the fireplace and scooped the ashes up with the fire-shovel, and putting it away for the night. Libby put the comb away and went to the door and bolted it. As she turned from the door, the light from the fire flared up, casting a shadow on the rough interior of the roof. She stopped suddenly!

"Is that ridgepole sagging?" she asked suddenly, "or am I seeing things?"

Joe looked up at the ridgepole. "You must be seeing things," he said teasingly. "It looks all right to me. Anyway, I'll put that pole up tomorrow since it seems to worry you." He went back and examined it. "It seems to be straight," he added.

In the uncertain light it was hard to tell. Libby gave a parting glance at the ridgepole and prepared for bed.

It was past midnight and Libby had not slept. She could hear the breathing of the two younger children in the trundle-bed below her. Occasionally one of the older girls in the bed at the opposite end of the room stirred in her sleep and called out as she did when at play.

Joe was dreaming of days on the battle field as the enemy advanced and his troops marched to form the battle-line, a resounding boom startled him into consciousness and he realized that he had been dreaming.

Libby shook his shoulder roughly. "Did you hear that noise?" she asked.

"I heard something that woke me up," said Joe. "I thought it was a cannon shot."

Libby sprang from her bed. "Quick! The post!" she cried. "It's the ridgepole!"

Joe was out of bed and into his clothes in a matter of seconds, like a fireman at a fire station.

Libby ran to the bed where the three older girls were sleeping.

"Lizzie!" she called, "get up and dress Hattie! And you, Clara, help Stella dress while I dress Eddie. We must get out of here!"

"Where are we going?" asked Clara, sleepily.

"Never mind, get dressed and don't ask questions! Hurry!"

Joe had left the door wide open when he went out, but now he came in dragging the heavy post. He laid it on the floor beneath the knot in the ridgepole and ran for a step-ladder and the scantling. Libby placed the ladder under the sagging ridgepole, which by now had a deep crack in it, and ran for a hammer and nails. Joe climbed the ladder and nailed the two-by-six to the under side of the ridgepole. With Libby's help, raised the post into its place and toe-nailed it fast to the scantling, as the five little half-dressed children clustered about them only partially visible in the flickering firelight.

Chapter 9

Deer Hunt

There was a skiff of snow on the ground, just enough to make tracking good. Will, putting the powder horn and hunting knife in his pocket, along with a few sandwiches, looped a rope around his waist in case he shot a deer that was too heavy to carry. He then slung the old army musket over his shoulder and was off for the first deer hunt of the season. The thermometer registered well below zero and the ice crackled under his heavy boots as he strode along towards the river. His idea was to cross the river and hunt on the north side among the hills.

The moon was still shining when he left the sod house before daylight, and although the sun came out later in the day the air was biting cold. He had been gone all day and as night came on, Joe and Libby watched anxiously for his return. Finally Libby spoke.

"A man could freeze to death in this cold," she said. Joe did not answer.

Darkness came on and still no dark figure could be seen coming up the trail from the river.

"Don't you think you'd better go down to the river and see if there is any sign of him?" asked Libby anxiously.

"O, he'll be all right," replied Joe. "He's been out in them hills before and knows every foot of that country. Just give him a little time and he'll make it back all right."

It was nearly midnight when Joe pulled on his boots and put on his mackinaw and mittens. Libby lit the lantern and handed it to him. Joe picked up a bundle of wood he had tied together with a rope, slung it across his shoulder and started out into the night.

"I'll build a fire on the bank of the river where he can see it if he's anywhere in the lower valley or on the river," he said.

As he approached the river he thought he could see a flicker of light either on the river or on the opposite bank. The light flared up, then died down again.

"It's a fire, but where is it?" he thought. With the lantern in his hand he climbed down the bank to the ice below.

"Something's happened or he would have come on home instead of building a fire." He stepped out on the ice. It was as solid as a concrete floor. "No chance of him falling in," he thought, "unless he's run into an air hole."

The firelight gleamed brighter as he came nearer to the middle of the stream. Now he was so near he could see that it was actually on the ice and about the middle of the river. What could this mean a fire on the ice? Didn't Will know better than to build a fire on ice?

As he approached the fire he could see a dark object. It was Will, apparently fast asleep. Joe knew it was not a natural sleep. He tried to rouse him but Will did not respond. He lifted the still form and placed it gently over his shoulder, but still no sign of life.

The river was wide and the ice slippery, but somehow Joe managed to reach the bank of the river. There he laid his burden on the frozen ground and began chafing Will's hands and moving his rigid body, but still there was no sign of consciousness. He laid his ear over the boy's heart. Yes, there was a faint heart-beat! Again he lifted the helpless body and with a great effort carried him to the door of the sod house.

Libby met them at the door and they laid Will on his bed. With trembling hands the frozen coat and ice-covered cap were removed. They tried to take off his boots, but found they were frozen stiff. Finally, the ice gave way and the boots came off, taking the skin with them.

"Did you get the deer?" he asked sleepily, "I hung it on a tree across the river."

"We'll see to that in the morning," replied his father, and Will turned his face to the wall and was soon fast asleep.

Will slept in late the next morning. When he finally awoke the deer was dangling from a tri-pod of pine-poles which Joe had taken from the woodpile.

"It sure is a dandy," said Joe as he drew his chair up beside Will's bed. "That'll keep us in meat for a long time. You did a mighty fine job of killing and dressing it. How on earth did you manage to bring it to the river and hang it up on that tree?"

"Well, to begin with," replied Will sleepily, "I left here about five o'clock in the morning, thinking I'd get across the river by the time the deer come down that way to feed. The moon was shining and deer like to feed by moonlight or early in the morning, so I thought I might find some down by the river among the willows."

Will was fully awake now and was sitting up in bed. He went on, "I knew there was a deer trail along the other side of the river and I followed that for awhile, but I didn't find any signs of deer, so I struck out to the northwest thinking if I'd pick up the trail they follow down to the river. Still I didn't see any traces and went on up into the hills."

"The ground was frozen as hard as a bullet, but I managed to walk without stepping on dry twigs. I thought sure there'd be a deer up there, but nothin' doin', so I went down the hill to the tail-end of the swale swamp. It's a big place down there and there are long runs of alders along the edge. I'd just gone out there where the grass had been knee-high before it snowed when something made me look up across the swale. I hadn't really heard any sound I guess, but there were something jumpin' stiff-legged down the hill. I wasn't sure they were within shootin' distance, but I fired anyhow and I saw the doe go down. She got up and I saw her limping down towards the river, so I knew I'd hit her. The buck turned north and disappeared in the brush."

"I stopped to load the old musket and the ramrod stuck in the barrel, but only for a second. I guess I was too excited even to load the gun right, but I soon had

Heading for Oregon

it loaded and was after the one I had shot. I tracked her for an hour or more, but didn't find hide nor hair of her. Of course, I hated to lose my deer after I'd shot it, but I hated worse to think of anything out in that cold suffering from a gun-shot wound."

By now Will was sitting on the edge of his bed with his bandaged feet on the floor.

"There's a cave up toward the rim-rock just at the edge of the divide," he continued. "I found it last summer when I was working at the Tom Wagoner ranch. They say Tom used to keep horses there when he brought them in from the range. That was before he built the stables on the island. I used to go up there and hunt grouse among the scrub pines in the hills. The boys at the ranch told about seeing deer around there in the winter. The cave's a fine place for deer to sleep as well as to hide in from hunters. Wild choke cherries and sand cherries grow all over them hills and the deer like the low brush they grow on. Up on the divide above the cave there's plenty of grass in summer. The snow wasn't too deep and I figured there was plenty of grass up there yet, so I took a chance of finding a deer up around the cave."

"I worked into the place slow and careful being as quiet as possible. There's a big rock just outside the mouth of the cave and I hid behind it and waited. From where I was hid I could see the whole hillside, except where the scrub pines were too thick and there, I calculated, was the place to keep my eyes glued."

"I must've set there an hour, or maybe two and didn't hear a sound except when a pine squirrel run out of his hole and barked at me. Then I heard a twig snap up on the hill a little way from the mouth of the cave. It's funny, Dad, how chilly it makes a feller feel just to hear a twig snap when you're huntin' deer. I froze my finger to the trigger of the musket and was trying to see through the underbrush. There was another crack, then sort of a rustling sound. I knew well enough there was a deer pokin' along in there, like a spook in the shadow, looking and listening and testing the air."

"For five minutes there wasn't a sound, then out of curiosity, I guess, a big buck poked his nose out of the brush and I fired away at him and down he went! He scrambled to his feet and stood there a few seconds just looking at me while I loaded the gun for a second shot, then he slumped to the ground and that time he didn't even try to get up. I cut his throat with the old toad stabber and dressed him out. I found I'd made a nice chest shot, missing his heart only a few inches. He's a six pointer and I guessed he'd weigh about a hundred and fifty pounds."

"I had forgotten all about lunch, but suddenly I remembered that I hadn't eaten anything since morning and then only a few bites, while I was getting ready to start. I took my sandwiches out of my slicker pocket and found they were frozen hard, but I was hungry enough to eat almost anything, so I swallowed them as fast as I could."

"I knew the deer was too heavy to carry, so I decided to drag him home on the snow. I hated to spoil his hide, so I took off my slicker coat and rolled him onto it and tied the rope around the butts of the horns. They're the prettiest rack I ever seen! I'm going to have 'em mounted."

"It was getting colder every minute and I knew that if I didn't get started soon it would be dark before I got home. I could hear the wolves howling in the hills and once I saw a gray shadow skulking along through the under brush. They smelled blood and it made them hungry, I guess. I didn't care to meet a bunch of them between there and the river with that deer dragging along behind me, so I decided to make tracks as fast as possible. I found a stick that made a good handle for the rope and tied it in and away I went."

"I hated to leave the cave for it was warmer in there than out in the cold wind. I was tempted to stay there all night, but I knew you and Mom would think something awful had happened to me, so I started out to drag the deer home. I was about four miles from the river and I was getting pretty cold. But, gee, was I hungry!"

"When I got to the river I was about all in. I decided to hang the deer in the big willow tree at the end of the trail and go home and come back in the morning to get him. I was so tired out by that time that I had a hard time getting the deer tied up in the tree, but I managed to get him up high enough to keep the wolves from getting at him. Then I made tracks for home."

"After I'd hung up the deer, I picked up some sticks of wood from under the old tree, thinking I'd make a fire when I got across the river to let you know where I was in case you was out looking for me and to get a little warm before I went on. I didn't get across the river though. I was so cold and tired I decided to build a fire on the ice. It's about two feet thick, you know."

"Yes, I know," replied his father. "It's a good thing you built that fire. If you hadn't you probably would still be out there on the ice."

"Well, when I got the fire built," continued Will, "and set down on the ice to rest I began to feel sleepy and for the life of me I couldn't keep my eyes open. My feet didn't seem as cold as they had been, but I began to feel numb all over. I guess if you hadn't found me when you did I'd've just set there and froze to death."

"You certainly would!" answered his father. "The thermometer registered forty below zero," he added, as he got up and strode to the fireplace.

"Forty below zero!" Will echoed.

"I've got one consolation," added Will, cheerfully, "we'll have plenty of venison to eat while I'm laid up with frozen feet."

Chapter 10

Father's Illness

"Inflammatory rheumatism," said Dr. Field, as he finished his diagnosis. "You'll be here flat on your back for a good many days. You've had too much strenuous exercise in this cold weather. You'd better go slow and stay close to the fire the rest of the winter. I'm not worrying about pay for my trip out here. What I am worrying about is your health and the welfare of your family. It was a long, cold trip I admit, but if I never get paid in this world I'll have something coming when I get to the next."

"It certainly was a hard trip, Dr. Field. Thirty-five miles in a blinding snowstorm with the temperature below zero is not fun," said Joe. "You're a brave man to undertake such a trip and for a penniless settler, to boot. That fire we had last summer left us nearly destitute, but you'll get your money somehow if I live long enough to earn it."

"What kind of a gun is that in the corner?" asked the doctor, picking up the old musket that leaned against the wall within arm's reach. "Of Civil War vintage, I'll be darned!" He took up the gun and examined it carefully. "I didn't get in on the big show," he said ruefully. "I was too young. I tried to enlist, but they turned me down."

"I carried that gun for three years," replied Joe, "and I wouldn't take anything for the experience that went with it. Thank goodness my life was spared and here I am living the life of a pioneer, suffering from exposure not only of this winter, but of the three winters and summers following General Johnson in his campaigns through the South."

"You're entitled to a pension, Joe. Have you ever applied for it?" asked the doctor.

The sick man raise himself on his elbow, his face flushed with fever and his eyes gleaming with a dull fire. "Dr. Field," he shouted, "I gave my services to my country and I hope never to have to ask for pay for what I did!" He lay back on the pillow, his features contorted and his hands clenched. "No sir! I'll never ask my Uncle Sam for a penny as long as I can crawl! Do you hear me? I'll starve before I'll beg for pay for what I volunteered to do for my country!"

Dr. Field saw that he had gone too far. "That's fine!" he said. "I'm proud of you. I like your grit. Do you think you could take some of this broth your wife has made for you?"

Joe sipped the broth from the spoon which Libby held in her trembling hand. "He's very nervous, you see," she said to the doctor.

"He'll need rest and quiet after the pain subsides," said the doctor. "I'll give him something to quiet his nerves and he'll go to sleep."

The doctor opened his case and took out some white tablets.

"Here, Joe," he said, "take this and you'll feel better. If you decide to apply for a pension just drop in at my office some time when you're in Sidney and I'll write up your application. It won't cost you a cent and a man like you deserves well of his country. I'll be glad to do anything I can to help you."

"Thank you, Doc.," said Joe, "I'll think it over."

"Libby, can you fix a place for the doctor to lie down and rest? He's had a long, cold ride in that little sleigh of his and needs rest as well as I do."

"Good night!" said the doctor as he lay down on the couch Libby prepared for him. "We'll both feel better in the morning after we've rested a few hours."

Chapter 11

Riding Jack, the Bay Mule

Jack, the bay mule, stood by the fence that enclosed the barn yard, looking towards the sod house. He saw his friend, twelve-year-old Clara coming down the path eating a big, red apple. As she came nearer Jack poked his black nose over the fence and gave a low "Hu, hu, hu!" which meant in mule language, "I'd like to have at least the core of that apple!"

Clara understood, and when she came near enough she held out what was left of the apple and Jack took it between his red lips and munched it as if he enjoyed it.

He knew Clara better than he did the other children of the family, because she often helped her father with the work outside. When they were through work Clara would help unhitch the mules and lead them to the watering trough before she led them to the stable where her father was pitching hay into their manger. Clara often brought him a cube of sugar or a piece of bread and he always thanked her by putting his nose on her shoulder and saying "Hu, hu, hu!"

After Jack had eaten the apple core he sidled up to the fence and Clara petted his neck and climbed up on his back.

Pete, the brown mule, didn't care as much for the children as Jack did, so he didn't get as many cubes of sugar and apple cores as Jack and that made him angry. As Clara rode around the corral, Pete turned his tail to them and looked in the opposite direction.

As they were coming back to their starting place, Clara saw Lizzie, her older sister, waiting for her.

"Let me ride!" called Lizzie, as Clara climbed down from Jack's back. "Maybe he'll let me ride this time. He tried to dump me off the last time I tried to ride him."

"You got a lump of sugar or anything for him to eat?" asked Clara. "He may not let you ride if you don't."

"No, I haven't anything for him," replied Lizzie, "but I'll try riding him anyhow."

Lizzie scrambled up on the high fence and Clara led Jack to where she could climb on his back. The mule looked at her as much as to say, "Haven't you even an apple core for me?"

"I haven't anything for you this time," said Lizzie, as if she understood mule language, "but maybe I'll think to bring you something next time."

She patted his neck as Clara had done, but Jack stood still for a minute then walked slowly around the corral.

Just as they were coming back Stella, the youngest of the three girls, ran around the corner of the stable. "I want to ride, too," she called.

"Well, climb up on the fence and get on behind me," said Lizzie as she drew Jack up close to the fence. Stella climbed on and both girls rode around the corral.

"That ain't fair!" exclaimed Clara. "Lizzie, you've had two rides to my one."

"Let's take him out to the back yard," said Lizzie, "and we'll all ride him."

"Not all at once," objected Clara. "He'll buck us off if we tease him too much."

"Naw, he won't," said Lizzie. "He's a good old mule. You won't buck us off, will you, Jack?"

Lizzie was more than a year older than Clara so she let Lizzie have her way, and, besides, Clara liked to ride as well as anybody.

Jack only shook his head a little. It was plain that he knew he was being imposed upon, but what could a mule do when a lot of kids didn't even understand when he tried to talk to them.

Lizzie led him by the halter, which he always wore when he wasn't hitched, up to the back yard where the grass was fresh and green. Perhaps, he thought, he might nibble a few mouthfuls of grass if he had time between rides.

"We can't ride him very many times," said Clara, "but maybe he'll stand it at least once."

Lizzie held Jack's halter as he nipped the tender grass while Clara ran to get an old sawhorse which stood behind the house. It was a heavy thing to carry, but she managed to drag it to a place near the mule where they could climb up on it and then onto Jack's back.

Stella ran for the old wooden stool which was outside the kitchen door.

"What are you going to do with that stool?" asked her mother from the open window.

Heading for Oregon

"O, nothing!" said Stella. "Just get up on Jack's back."

"You'd better be careful how you ride that mule," said her mother. "He'll dump you all off some of these days."

Stella was around the corner of the house by that time and didn't answer.

They led Jack to the sawhorse and put the stool beside it so they could climb up. Clara climbed on first, for she was used to driving Jack, then Lizzie helped Stella up and then scrambled up herself.

Jack stood patiently until all three were settled on his back. Clara patted his neck. "Getty up, Jack," she said, but the mule didn't budge.

"Go on, old fellow," coaxed Lizzie.

Jack laid back his big ears, but didn't move. "Go on!" she urged and at the same time dug her heels into his flanks.

This time Jack moved, but in the wrong direction. With his ears laid back, he put his head down between his front legs and kicked up his heels and the three little girls slid over his head in a squirming, screaming heap on the grass. Jack ran kicking and squealing across the yard, then turned back to look at them. His big, red lips were drawn back in a broad grin as though he were enjoying the trick he had played on them.

"He-haw, he-haw!" he brayed as he ran out to the pasture back of the stable as much as to say, "I've had enough of your foolishness. You didn't even give me a lump of sugar or an apple core, nor thank me for the other rides you had in the corral. Goodbye! The next time, treat a mule right and he'll treat you right."

Chapter 12

Eddie and the Rattle Snake

"I don't see why babies have to come right in the middle of summer," Clara said to herself, "leastways, right in hayin' time. Ma's been gone three weeks now and I think it's about time she's comin' home."

Clara was her father's helper when her brother, Will, was away from home as he had been most of the summer. She had been raking hay all morning and was tired.

Her father was at the well pumping water for the mules. The clear water trickled merrily down the trough to the larger trough where Jack and Pete were drinking, takin long, deep draughts of the cool water.

Clara had helped her father unhitch the mules and was laying up the bars of the barnyard fence when a man rode up to the well and spoke to her father.

"It's a ten-pound boy," he announced. "Your wife can come home any time now. I'll be there for awhile and Mrs. Radcliffe thinks we can get along. Mac, her husband, you know, had to go out on the roundup. Nobody knows where the crew is, but everything's okay anyhow. I'da brought your wife home, but we couldn't both leave at the same time."

"We'll manage somehow to get her home. Thanks for letting me know," said Joe, as the rider wheeled his horse and rode back across the sand hills towards Cedar Creek ranch.

Joe stood for a minute thinking. He had been mowing all morning and had a lot of hay down. He should work at that this afternoon. He turned and walked into the house. Stella was placing the last plate on the dinner table and Lizzie was lifting the meat from the kettle with a big fork as he came into the kitchen. Dinner was steaming hot as Joe liked it to be. The girls had done mighty well since their mother had been away, he thought.

"Who was that man here a minute ago?" asked Clara, coming in from the corral. She threw her broad-brimmed hat on the bed as she reached for the wash pan.

"Will Moore from the Cedar Creek ranch," replied her father. "Mrs. Radcliffe has a new baby and Will came to tell us your mother could come home any time now."

"O, goody! Goody! "Ma's comin' home! Ma's comin' home!" squealed five-year-old Hattie hopping around the dinner table on one foot.

"Well, let's eat," said Joe, seating himself at the table. The children were all too excited to eat much and the meal was soon finished.

"Are you goin' after Ma today?" asked Clara, twisting her tongue around the last bite.

"I've just been thinking about it," said Joe. "How would you like to take the new hay rake and go after her? We'll hitch Jack to the rake and your mother can ride on the frame. It won't be a very good place to ride," he said thoughtfully. "I'd take the team and go after her myself, but I've just got to keep at that hay or it'll be spoiled."

"Sure, I'd like to go!" exclaimed Clara. "Goody! I'm glad she's comin' home, and I'll get to see the new baby, too, before the rest of you kids," she chuckled. "How soon can I go, Pa?"

"Right away," replied her father, "and the sooner the better. It's five miles up there and it'll be getting dark before you get back. I'll hitch Jack to the rake while you get ready."

"I want to go, too!" wailed Eddie. "I want to see my mamma!" he pleaded, tears coming to his brown eyes.

"Can't I take him, Pa?" coaxed Clara. "We can fix a nice seat for him on one side of the rake and tie him in so he can't fall off. Please, Pa, he wants to go!"

"I guess he'll be all right," said Joe. "Lizzie, you clean him up a bit while Clara changes her dress. I'll hitch up the mule and you can start before I go back to the hay field."

Joe took an armful of gunny sacks from a peg in the stable and fastened them to the chassis of the hay rake with a rope, then looped a strap around one of the crossbars so that it would be handy when Eddie was ready to be tied on. "It'll be safe that way," he thought.

Clara and Eddie were ready by the time Joe had the mule hitched to the rake. "OK!" he called. "Who's for the coach ride?"

Clara lifted Eddie up to the seat which Joe had made for him and he was strapped securely to the crossbar. He looked very uncomfortable.

Heading for Oregon

"He'll ride there all right," said Joe.

Clara climbed to the high, red seat of the new rake, and her father handed her the lines. She felt very important at being allowed to drive that far all by herself.

"Be careful," her father said with a twinkle in his brown eyes, "and don't run over any prairie dogs or rattle snakes. You might hurt them." And, he added in a more serious tone, "don't let Jack step in a prairie-dog hole. Get back as soon as you can," he continued, somewhat anxiously.

"Here we go on the tallyho!" called Clara as she slapped the lines on old Jack's back. The girls waved to them from the door of the sod house and Eddie waved back, and then grabbed nervously at the strap that held him to the frame of the rake. He didn't feel too safe perched there on the iron crossbar.

Joe turned to Lizzie. "Can you girls clean up the house a bit before your mother comes home?" he asked them.

"Sure! We can clean up the house!" said Lizzie, looking at her father almost reproachfully.

"And I'll help!" chimed in Stella.

"Me, too!" echoed Hattie. "I can dry the dishes."

Clara cut across the prairie-dog town west of the house. That was much nearer than going around by the road and almost as good traveling. She entered the main road as she neared the sand hills, plowing through the loose sand nearly to the hubs of the rake wheels. She recalled her father's warning about the prairie-dogs and the rattlesnakes. "Anyhow," she thought, "we're past the prairie-dog town and there's no chance of running over one of them dogs now, and Jack didn't step in one of the holes, either."

Perched on the high seat and holding the lines back over Jack's shining bay coat she looked straight ahead, keeping her eyes on the road, but glancing at Eddie now and then to see that he hadn't fallen off. His red head seemed to be passing the spoke of the wheel and reminded her of little red pigs running past a picket fence.

Suddenly Eddie called out, pointing towards the rim of the wheel just above his head, "O, look! Look! Siser! It sees me! It sees me!"

Startled, Clara glanced in the direction in which he was pointing. "Horrors!" she screamed as she saw the object at which the child was looking.

At the top of the wheel was a huge rattler coiled several times around the rim, its shining, diamond-shaped head thrust out towards the child on the chassis of the rake, its beady eyes glittering and its forked tongue darting in and out between its wide-open jaws.

In desperation Clara struck the unsuspecting mule with the lines with a resounding whack and he started in a run down the steep hill, the rake swaying crazily from side to side in the loose sand as he ran. Eddie hung on to the crossbar with all his might. Clara watched the snake and trusted to the mule to go in the right direction. The wheels spun round so rapidly she could scarcely see the spokes. Round and round they flew, the snake still clinging desperately to the rim. Suddenly it let go and fell off.

"It's gone!" cried Eddie. "I wanted to keep it!"

Heading for Oregon

Clara paid no attention to what he was saying. Her whole body was quivering, and she felt as though she would fall off the high seat. She could scarcely hold the lines in her trembling hands. "Whoa!" she called to the frightened mule and drew the lines tighter. The mule, feeling the pressure of the lines on his back gradually slowed down to a walk.

They reached the ranch house and Clara climbed down from her lofty perch and was unstrapping Eddie from the crossbar, when her mother came out ready to go home. As she kissed her daughter she noticed that she was pale and trembling.

"What's the matter Clara?" she asked. "You're shaking all over and you look pale. What's happened?"

"Nothing," replied Clara. "I'm kinda tired. I've been raking hay all morning."

"A pitty thing was on the wheel!" said Eddie, "and Jack runned away."

"Nothing!" said his mother, looking at Clara. "Nothing!"

As she turned to drive out to the road, Clara remembered that she hadn't seen the new baby after all.

Near the top of the hill lay a dead rattle snake. "There it is, Mommy! There it is!" shouted Eddie, pointing.

"Hush!" said his mother, holding her baby close to her heart, but Clara was looking straight ahead and didn't seem to see the dead rattle snake.

Chapter 13

Willis Court and His Eye for the Girls

"I'll shoot the man that molests one of my girls!" Libby's brown eyes snapped as she watched her thirteen-year old daughter, Lizzie, struggling to free herself from the embrace of Willis Court, a young man who had been hanging around the settlement for more than a year. He had filed on the quarter section east of the Kirkpatrick place and had built a sod house. Meanwhile he slept in a pup-tent, which he called his dog house, and prepared his frugal meals over an open camp fire.

Libby was standing in the door of her sod house. She stepped back into the house and reached for a revolver which lay on the mantle of the fireplace. Lizzie scrambled down from her perch on the seat of the wagon in the shade of the stable where she had taken refuge from the sun that hot afternoon in July.

"Aw, come now, honey," drawled Willis. "I won't hurt you. Come back little girlie. Can't you be friendly with your neighbor?"

Ignoring his plea, Lizzie ran to the house and entered the door where her mother had stood a moment before. Without a word to the girl, Libby appeared in the doorway, the revolver concealed in the fold of her gingham dress. That was the second time that insolent intruder had taken undue advantage of her eldest daughter, and Libby resented it bitterly.

"I didn't even know he was there till he put his arm around me," panted the girl. "He must've climbed in at the back of the wagon. I hate 'im, Ma! I don't want 'im to come near me! I hate 'im, I hate 'im I say!" and her slender, brown fingers covered her gray eyes as she burst into angry tears.

"You stay here, Lizzie," said her mother. "I'll have a word with this young rascal, myself. There are too many tales afloat about Willis Court and the girls of this community knew."

This gentle little woman was an infuriated tigress when the honor of her daughter was at stake. With the gun still concealed in the folds of her full skirt Libby stepped out into the path that led to the stable.

She ran to the opposite side of the wagon, but the culprit had disappeared. She hurried to the back of the stable and could see him making long strides down the rows of corn in the direction of his pup-tent, half a mile distant. He glanced back over his shoulder occasionally as he strode forward, but did not pause as Libby stood watching him. "I'll tell that young man what I think of him when I see him again," she muttered between clenched teeth.

Only the day before Libby and Joe had returned from Sidney whence they had been summoned as witnesses in the case in which Bertie Mormon, a neighbor girl, was being asked to identify the father of her new-born babe. Willis Court had been named as defendant and had been found guilty.

Where Willis Court had come from was a mystery. He would drop into the settlement, stay for a few days at his camp, then disappear as mysteriously as he had come, leaving not trace of where he had gone nor why he had come. His straight, black hair was always neatly parted in the middle and roached back above well-formed ears. His narrow, black brows were easily puckered into a frown when he was displeased, or raised suggestively at a questionable remark. He had a way of passing his sharp-pointed tongue nervously over his thin, red lips. There was a peculiar, indefinable something about him which Libby had detested from the time he first appeared in the neighborhood. She disliked and distrusted him. His beady, black eyes had a way of shifting uneasily when he was talking, although he seldom had anything of importance to say. He had won the favor of a few of the younger women of the settlement, particularly of the Mormon family. Many a free meal and night's lodging were the result, in addition to the birth of Bertie's illegitimate child.

Chapter 14

The Day Lighting Struck Zena Dead!

Joe had gone to Sidney to lay in supplies for the coming hay harvest. He was expected home that night. Andy Johnson and Zena Webb were already at the house ready to begin mowing.

The black thunder cloud bore down upon them as the two men hitched their horses to the mower. It had taken them all morning to get ready for the big job and they were anxious to at least get under way that afternoon.

Libby stood in the doorway of the sod house, watching the storm approach. She stepped out into the yard to get a better view of the oncoming cloud and noticed that the men were hitching their team to the mower. "Don't you think you'd better wait till the storms over before you begin mowing?" she asked tall, freckled faced Johnson. "There's too much danger working with a sickle during a thunderstorm."

Andy glanced at his companion, a tall, handsome young man who had come with him to help through harvest. "I guess we'll have to humor her," he said aside to his companion. "Women are worrisome, but Libby Kirk's got a lot of good sense an' mebby she's right, after all."

Reluctantly the two men unhitched their horses and led them into the sod stable as the storm advanced.

Flashes of lightning blinded them for an instant and the rolling thunder made the tense air vibrate. They tied the horses in their stalls and Andy ran to the house. Zena stood in the stable door, his hands resting on either side of it.

As Andy reached the house, hailstones the size of goose eggs began to fall, making a thudding sound on the hard-baked ground. He stood in the doorway and watched the storm. Libby and the children took refuge on the feather bed in the opposite corner of the room. Crash after crash rocked the earth and flashes of lightning followed each other in quick succession.

From the door Andy shouted, "Mrs. Kirk, the lightning struck in front of the stable an' I believe it killed a hen. I saw something black bounce up in front of the stable door!"

"Where's Zena?" exclaimed Libby.

"I left him in the stable," shouted Andy, trying to make himself heard above the roar of the storm.

"Go, quick, and see if he's all right!" said Libby, running to the door.

Andy pulled his cap down over his eyes and ducked his head to avoid the fast-falling hailstones. He ran to the stable and entered its low door, and lying flat on his back Zena sprawled on the earthen floor! His felt hat, with a patch of singed hair on the inner band lay a few feet farther back in the stable. A burnt streak passed down his white forehead, down the bridge of his nose and lengthwise of the adamsapple. The odor of burnt flesh was sickening.

Andy turned and fled to the house. "Zena's dead! Zena's dead!" he shouted. "Get me the camphor!"

Snatching the camphor bottle from Libby's hand, Andy rushed back to the stable, closely followed by Libby and her twelve-year old daughter Clara. In his frenzy Andy poured camphor down the throat of the lifeless boy.

With trembling hands, Andy and Libby assisted by the frightened Clara, lifted the lifeless form and carried it into the house. They laid him gently on the homemade bed in the corner of the room and covered him with a sheet.

Andy rode to the camp of some men who had pitched their tent by the river, preparatory to mowing the hay on a quarter-section along the river bank. Two men rode back to the sod house with him and stayed that night with the unhappy family.

Joe returned late that night. The next day Zena Webb was placed tenderly in the back of Andy's wagon and taken to his home on the Divide.

Chapter 15

Hattie Shot!

"One, two, three, down I go!" Hattie slid down the smooth board and landed in the loose sand at the foot of it.

"One, two, fee, down I goes!" Eddie followed her and almost lit on top of her at the end of the board.

The north side of the sod house was the coolest places to be found on the sun-baked claim that sweltering afternoon in early fall. Joe had brought a wagon load of fine, white sand from the river and dumped it right there where the children could play in it from morning until night. Then he planed a long foot board and placed the end of it securely on the sill of the low north window where the children could play to their hearts content. It was such fun to slide down the long, smooth board, and land at the foot of it, half buried in the sand.

Their laughter resounded through the house and echoed against the hard, dry ridgepole which extended from end to end of the sod house.

"It's my turn, now," said Hattie, and flash of blue calico went gliding down the smooth board and the child sprang nimbly to her feet as she struck the sand. She brushed the dust from her auburn hair and dark brown eyes and ran back to the window.

"Now, it's your turn!" said Hattie, her voice rang out clear and sweet. "I'll help you up," and the older sister by sixteen months gave her four-year old brother a boost to the window sill. He straddled the long board and went flying to the opposite end.

And so they played for hours at a time, up to the window and down to the sand pile until beads of perspiration stood on their flushed foreheads and rolled down rosy cheeks.

"I'm tired now. I can't slide any more," said Hattie, out of breath. "Let's rest awhile."

"I'm not tired!" echoed Eddie, and slid the length of the board again, while Hattie, weary but happy, climbed through the low window to the coolness of the interior of the sod house. She looked through the door at the opposite end of the one-room house and saw her father and Will drive up at the farther end of the hard-packed yard. They had been to the river to get another load of sand. This was to be scattered on the surface of the chicken yard.

Will swung down from the wagon seat and picked up his twenty-two rifle from the bottom of the wagon bed. He had taken it with him to the river in the hopes that he might find a duck or a rabbit.

"Is that gun loaded?" called his mother from near the well where she was dipping water from a tub which had been placed under the spout of the pitcher pump. She was preparing to water the *Four-O'clocks* which were the only flowers she had been successful in growing in that hot climate where water could scarcely be spared for flowers.

"No, mother, this gun is not loaded!" Will's voice expressed annoyance. He had been asked that question so often that he resented it. "See!" he said as he pointed the gun downward and pulled the trigger.

A flash! A crash! And a child's scream from inside the house were simultaneous. Will stood dumfounded while the gun smoking in his hands.

Libby rushed into the house, lifted the still form of her little girl from the floor and carried her to the tub of water by the well, the blood streaming down over the child's face.

Will slammed the rifle down into the wagon box and ran to his mother's side. "Is she dead?" he whispered.

But Libby did not answer. "Get me a towel," she said as she washed the blood from Hattie's face.

The wound was in the forehead, and Libby wrapped the towel about the head of the crying child. She sat on the well platform praying that the precious life may be spared. Will covered his face with his hands and leaned his head against the wall of the sod house and sobbed.

The wound proved to be scalp wound about the middle of the forehead. A few hours later Hattie smiled through swollen eyelids and said, "Ma held me on her lap an' thought I was gonna die, but I kept wight on wivin."

Will went to the wagon where the gun was still lying. "How on earth could the bullet have struck her when the muzzle of the gun was pointed down?" he asked himself. With gun in hand he went down the path to the house. About half way between the wagon and the house he found a deep scar in the hard surface of the path where the bullet had struck and glanced upward. A dent was found in the ridgepole of the house. The spent bullet had glanced down from there and truck Hattie in the middle of the forehead.

Chapter 16

Tom Wagoner

"Hey, Red, come out here!" Tom Wagoner's burly form appeared around the corner of the sod stable. He leaned slightly forward, his heavy jaw extended and ruddy lips drawn back over white teeth. In his hand he carried a wicked-looking whip of braided cowhide thongs, the butt loaded with lead.

Red's stalky figure emerged through the stable door, his dark, red hair gleaming in the morning sun.

"So you're tellin' the kid about our trip last week! I heard you," snarled Tom. "You can't keep nothin' to yourself, from now on keep your mouth shut! Take that!" Tom brought the heavy whip-lash down across Red's shoulders.

"If I'll take that from any man!" muttered Red between set teeth, and he struck out fiercely at Tom with a hairy, clinched fist.

With the lithe movement of a cat, Tom stepped aside and avoided the blow. "I'll give you to understand, young feller, that the guys around this ranch don't discuss my business," said Tom, his black eyes flashing angrily. "Keep that in mind hereafter."

Red's only reply was the curl of his rough, red bearded upper lip.

"After this, continued Tom, "you stay on the island. Ya hear me? You'll find plenty to do there an' nobody

Heading for Oregon

to talk to but them horses we fetched in yesterday. I'm goin' over to the island now, so pile on that Cayuse. Saddle old Sandy for me an' we'll get goin'."

Tom's meaning was clear to Red, a burly Irish ranch hand. For the hands to discus Tom's business was not as uncommon as Tom may have thought, but they usually got away with it without being caught.

Tom had taken Red with him on a trip the week before. Starting shortly after dark they had traveled all night and slept in a canyon miles away, the next day. Early the next evening, they had rounded up a band of horses which Tom claimed to have bought and returned to the Wagoner ranch with them the next morning. The "receivin' stables," as Tom called them, were a group of sod buildings on a long island which extended lengthwise of the North Platte River south of Tom's main ranch. These stables were cleverly concealed among the willows which grew abundantly on the island.

Red saddled and bridled the horses; the two men mounted them and without a word rode in the direction of the river. At the bank they dismounted, tied their horses among the willows, stepped into a small rowboat and paddled across the channel to the island.

"This is a good place for a bunch of new horses," remarked Tom "They can't stray away from here unless they swim the river, an' horses don't like to swim unless they have to."

"They swum over here last night," retorted Red.

"Yeah, I know, but they had to swim or feel the bite of this whip," replied Tom, defiantly snapping the whip which he habitually carried.

Red's blue eyes flashed, but he made no reply. He still felt the sting of that whip across his shoulders.

"Go an' git them brandin' irons," commanded Tom, "then make a fire out there among them willers. We gotta brand all these horses while we're at it."

Red obeyed silently, cursing under his breath.

At noon they were joined by a crew of men from the ranch. For hours they worked, heating branding irons over red-hot coals, lariating the horses, throwing them to the ground, roping their legs together, obliterating the brands of former owners and burning the brand of the Tom Wagoner ranch on their sensitive skins. The odor of burning hair and horse flesh drifted down the broad river.

Occasionally a man would recognize a brand as that of a rancher for whom he had worked. He would point to the brand, wink at his companion and go on with his work without a word.

Tom mingled with his men as much as possible, giving sharp orders and seeing that they were carried out without comment.

By nightfall the job of branding was completed. Before leaving the island he called Red to the sod hut in which he was to live while on the island. "You know your job," Tom said. "If you see any strangers tryin' to ford the south channel use this," and he pointed significantly at a rifle which leaned against the wall in a corner of the hut.

"Sure, I know my job!" snapped Red. "Leave it to me!"

"I'll leave it to you!" retorted Tom. "And mind how you use that rifle."

Red's bullet head bobbed in response, but a deeper crimson mounted his freckled face.

Tom and his crew paddled back across the channel, mounted their horses and returned to the ranch, all but Red, who was left alone on the island, awaiting further orders.

Mystery concealed the sudden disappearance of the big, burly Irishman. When the men returned to the island next morning Red was nowhere to be found. One of the best horses was gone and the rifle which Tom had left with him had also disappeared.

Chapter 17

Frank and the Rattler!

Frank, the black and tan shepherd dog, lay outside the kitchen door, his head slightly raise and eyes alert, ready for any adventure. It might be a run after the cow or a romp in the tall grass with the children. Joe was proud of that dog because he was so helpful with the stock. Libby trusted him because of his fine intelligence and his watchful care over the children when they were out playing about the place. They all loved him because he was a faithful friend to every member of the family. Hattie and Eddie, the two younger children, were his special care. When they went out to play in the tall grass which crept up to the very walls of the sod house Frank ran ahead of them, sniffing about and examining every unusual object until he was satisfied that all was safe for his little charges. Then he would curl himself up in a furry ball near them, his bright eyes noting their every movement.

Frank did not quiet Libby's desperate fear of rattlesnakes completely, for her fears were well grounded, for snakes were plentiful in the valley. Joe had killed one between the house and the stable, and another had been found in the chicken yard that very spring. All this Libby knew well, but she also knew that it was impractical to keep the children in the

Heading for Oregon

house all the time. They had been indoors so much during the long, cold winter that they were beginning to look pale. It seemed essential to their good health for them to play out in the sunshine after the long winter was over. She was grateful that Frank did seem to sense the danger somewhat. She thought that was why he guarded the children so carefully.

"Yes, you may go out for a little while, but don't stay too long," Libby said one morning in early spring as she tied the strings of Hattie's little pink sunbonnet under the dimpled chin. "Here, Eddie, is your cap. Be sure to keep it on your head. The sun is hot and you will sunburn if you don't wear it." She kissed the rosy faces and sent the children out to play.

As she turned to go in she saw Frank at her side wagging his tail; his brown eyes were shining with eager anticipation. "Yes, Frank, go with them and take good care of my babies," she said. Frank bounded after the children, as glad as they were to be out in the sunshine. Libby breathed a prayer for the children's safety as she watched them. Eddie was chasing a butterfly, his tiny figure darting in and out among the tall grasses in his effort to capture the flitting bit of color. His bright red hair peeped from beneath the blue cap and lay in damp ringlets on his forehead. Hattie had found some small sticks of wood and was building a tiny pig pen among the tall grasses. Libby felt that the children were comparatively safe so long as he was with them.

She went back into the kitchen. There were dishes to wash and the floor to sweep; there were numberless little socks and dresses to be mended. Hers was a busy life, and no mistake, looking after such a large family in a pioneer home. The breakfast dishes were stacked in the big tin dishpan which stood on the kitchen table. As she lifted the steaming teakettle from the sheet-iron camp stove and began to pour hot water over the dishes, she heard a slight rustling sound. It startled her! She turned quickly, set the kettle on the stove, and ran toward the door. By that time she could detect light footsteps trotting briskly up the path, and before she could reach the door Frank was at her side, pulling at the hem of her gingham dress. He was whining softly, almost pleadingly, it seemed to Libby. A grim sense of danger tugged at her heart. "My babies!" she thought. "What has happened to them? Frank, where are the children? Hurry, take me to them!"

Still holding to the hem of her dress, Frank led her swiftly through the open door. Loosening his teeth from her dress he ran ahead of her down the path toward the stable, frequently glancing back, apparently to assure himself that she was following him. In the blazing sun stood the two children, looking intently at a slender object stretched at full length and lying motionless in the pathway along which they must have passed but a few minutes before. It had diamond-shaped figures on its back and Libby recognized it as an unusually large prairie rattlesnake. She noticed a few small sticks and some pebbles lying in the path near it.

Libby's heart stood still! What could she do? If either she or one of the children should move the venomous beast might coil and strike and both of the children were within striking distance! Her blood ran cold. "Stand still!" she called to them. Neither of the children moved. Even the dog seemed transfixed. He stood by Libby's side, his nose pointing directly at the snake, his tail pointing in the opposite direction and his back and neck bristling.

Fearing to move, even to go around the snake to where the children stood, Libby gazed in terror at the hateful object. Then she discovered something unusual about it. Near its middle was a big large lump, as large as a man's fist. A sluggish appearance was in the staring eyes, not the usual glitter peculiar to the eyes of most snakes. Frequently its tail moved slowly from side to side and there was an occasional convulsive movement of its throat as though it were trying to swallow something. She could see that it had a long string of rattles.

Suddenly she was startled by a rushing movement. A black and tan streak flashed past her and Frank had the reptile by the back of the neck, shaking it furiously the rattles making a slight rasping sound as they rubbed together. Then flinging it from him with all his strength, he trotted a few steps toward his mistress, paused and instant and turned to look at his victim now lying some ten feet away on the hard ground.

A large, brown toad was seen hopping slowly toward the stable door where it sat in the shade, blinking its big eyes stupidly. Evidently it had not enjoyed being a Jonah in the belly of a snake.

It was all done so quickly that Libby scarcely realized what had happened. She stood like one paralyzed.

Suddenly, however, she was running down the path where the snake had so recently lain and clasped the two children in her arms. " Thank Heaven, you are safe!" she sobbed as she held them close to her heart and kissed them again and again.

"I frowed sticks at it," ventured Hattie.

"Yes, I saw the sticks," said her mother.

"Me fwoed wocks," chimed in Eddie. "See my flutterby," he added, opening his chubby fist in which lay a crumpled bit of color. Libby kissed him again with tears in her eyes.

Frank came and stood by Libby's side, looking wistfully up into her face, his brown eyes seeming to say, "I did it for you as well as for your babies." Libby's hand caressed the dog's velvety ears as hot tears coursed down her pale cheeks. "You're a treasure!" she sobbed.

Chapter 18

School Days

Before the summer was ended, the little community in Weir valley had organized a Sunday school which met in a small frame building near the Bateman home. About thirty people attended and took part in the services. Joe Kirkpatrick was chosen as superintendent.

In the meantime efforts were made to establish a school district. This was accomplished before Christmas. Mr. Bateman was elected chairman of the school board and John Carlson and Joe were also members of the board.

It was a cold morning in December when Joe mounted his bay mule and rode to the Bateman place to look over the building. As he neared the wooden structure he could hear singing.

Joy to the world, the Lord has come!
Let earth receive her king!

The clear, girlish voice rang out on the frosty air as Joe dismounted the mule. He threw the bridle-rein over the hitching-post near the door and stopped to listen, his dark eyes shining with approval. The sound of an organ accompanied the girl's voice and reverberated on the crisp winter air.

The singing suddenly ceased and Joe heard the same voice speaking. "Sing, Heuy, sing!" the girl was saying.

"Aw, I don't wanna," came a lisping, childish voice.

"Oh, come on, Huey!" coaxed the girl. "You know Mr. Kirk wanted all of us to sing these songs at the Christmas tree next Sunday."

Joe stepped to the little wooden platform which served as a porch in front of the door and stood there for a moment. So as not to disturb the singer, he quietly stamped the snow from his heavy boots and brushed away the frost from his black mustache.

"OK, Sis," came the boy's voice. "If Joe Kirk wanths me to thing this thong I'll try it. He's thupertendent of the Thunday School an' the best guy in this whole country," and the childish voice took up the well-known refrain and sang it out lustily.

Maggie had won, as she usually did, when dealing with her young brother. She had a way with children; a gentle but persuasive way, which pleased Joe greatly as he stood there listening.

"She'll do," he said to himself. "She's only sixteen, but she knows how to get youngsters to do what she wants them to do."

Maggie and Huey were so intent on their singing that they did not see Joe as he entered the room. He had time to look over the meagerly furnished interior. A wood fire crackled in a small heater which stood at one side of the room and the red embers glowed warmly through the iron wall of the stove from which ashes trickled through to the hard dirt floor. Half a dozen rough benches were arranged in the middle of the room and a rough, hand-made desk stood facing them at the farther end of the room. Back of the desk on a tipsy-looking tripod rested a rectangular piece of blackboard and a box of yellow chalk stood on the floor beside it.

A small Esty organ with yellowing keys and lusterless cabinet stood between the desk and the stove. The tones of the organ were good and Maggie played, not too skillfully, but well enough for the pioneers to sing by in the little Sunday school.

Maggie sat on the wobbly organ stool, her brown fingers gliding lovingly over the yellow keys. A stream of sunlight fell across the slender figure, lighting up the mass of golden brown hair which was drawn smoothly back from the finely-featured face and hung in two shining braids over her slender shoulders. Her red lips were compressed into a straight line in her effort to play the organ and at the same time to induce Huey to sing. It was no easy task.

Huey, short and stocky, with tussled, tawny hair, stood beside the organ, singing the carol with all the vehemence of his sturdy young voice.

"Fine, fine!" exclaimed Joe as the strains of the notes died away.

"Did you hear me thing?" shouted Huey. "I'm a gonna thing at the Christmas tree."

"Sure, I heard you sing," answered Joe. "We all want to hear you sing, and you can do it, too."

Maggie whirled round on the organ stool at the sound of Joe's voice, her face crimson under its coat of tan, her blue eyes greeting Joe frankly, but modestly.

"We're practicing for the Christmas program," she explained. "Huey thought at first that he couldn't sing, but I guess he's decided he can; anyway, he's going to try."

"You're doing fine," said Joe, "and so is Huey. We'll have a good program and no mistake."

In a more serious tone he added, "Miss Maggie, how would you like to teach our school next spring?" Huey slid out through the door. He is not interested in schools.

Maggie's smooth brow contracted. "Why, why!" she stammered. "Why, Mr. Kirk, I don't know how to teach school. I never taught in my life."

"The school board had a meeting last night," continued Joe. "Your father is chairman of the board, you know. Didn't he tell you we talked of asking you to teach the spring term?"

"No-o!" replied Maggie. "I heard him tellin' Ma they had decided to have a three-month term if they could afford to hire a teacher, but I didn't hear him say anything about me teaching."

"Just like Jim," said Joe. "He said last night that you were too young to teach school and that he didn't think you could get a certificate before you were eighteen. That was the law where you came from, and beside, he thought you didn't have enough schooling to teach anybody. But I think you can do it. John Carlson is the other director and Jim left it to us to decide. John and I talked it over and decided that if you wanted to try it we'd hire you."

"O, Mr. Kirk," gasped Maggie. "I'd be scared to death to try it."

"We haven't much money to pay a teacher," continued Joe. "At the meeting last night we decided to levy a tax, but we won't get that before next fall and we ought to have school next spring. My youngsters are running wild and ought to be in school."

"So's ours," replied Maggie.

"I went to the county superintendent," Joe went on, and found there was very little money in the treasury for us. All we can pay you is ten dollars a month for three months."

Maggie's mathematical mind was at work. "Three months at ten dollars a month," she calculated. "Why, that's thirty dollars! I've not seen that much money since we came here." Her blue eyes shone with anticipation, "a new dress for me and some new shoes for Ma!"

"Think it over," said Joe, "and let me know tomorrow. Will you?"

"I already thought it over," replied Maggie promptly. "It's not every day I can get thirty dollars and I'm not going to miss this chance!"

"You'll have to have a permit," said Joe.

"What's a permit?" queried Maggie vaguely.

"It's a license to teach for a short time," replied Joe.

"O!" said Maggie.

"You can get it by going to the county superintendent's office in Sidney," replied Joe. "He'll give you some kind of an examination, I suppose, and if you can pass that he will give you a permit to teach in this county until the next regular examination, which will be in the fall."

"Good! I'll get to go to Sidney again," said Maggie, her eyes dancing. "I've not been in town since last summer."

"Its thirty-five miles to Sidney, you know," said Joe, "and it's mid-winter. School should begin about the first of April, but you'll have to get your permit before that time. We'll hope for good weather."

"Pa's going to Sidney as soon as the weather's fit," said Maggie, "and I can go with him and get my permit then."

"I'm glad to hear you say that," said Joe. "I think you'll make us a good teacher. Work hard on your language so you can talk up to the superintendent."

"You bet I will!" replied Maggie.

"Well, I must be getting back home. The fires'll be out. They take a lot of wood these days," said Joe.

"They sure do," replied Maggie. "Thanks a lot for asking me to teach school. I think it'll be a bushel of fun."

"I'm the one to thank you for accepting the offer," replied Joe, as he mounted the bay mule and rode homeward.

The next Sunday afternoon the rafters of the little frame building rang with carols led by Joe and accompanied on the organ by Maggie. Huey's voice could be heard above the others,

"Joy to the world, the Lord haths come!"

Teachers were scarce and Maggie found no difficulty in securing a permit to teach. There were only five pupils in the school: the three older Kirkpatrick girls, Lizzie, Clara and Stella, and Maggie's two brothers, Wesley and Huey. Miss

Maggie, as she insisted upon having her pupils call her, proved to be a conscientious teacher and won the respect and affection of her pupils and the neighborhood alike. The three spring months sped merrily by and the school closed with a program on the evening of the last day.

The little platform was gaily decorated with streamers and rosettes of bright-colored crepe paper and Joe's tattered Civil War flag graced the center of the miniature stage.

Miss Maggie announced the program and Huey was the first to be called. He marched boldly to the wooden platform and recited:

> "Tell me not in mournful numbers
> Life is but an empty dweam,
> For the thoul ith dead that thlumberths
> And things are not what they theem.
>
> In the worlths bwoad field of battle,
> In the bigwhack of life
> Be not like dumb, dwiven cattle;
> Be a he-o in the stwife.

The audience applauded and Huey ran triumphantly to his seat.

"You forgot to make your bow!" said his mother.

"I sure did!" said Huey, and he ran back to the stage and made an elaborate bow amid the laughter of the crowd and then ran back to his seat.

Stella sat beside her mother on a wooden bench awaiting her turn to speak. Then Miss Maggie called her name.

Like a flash Stella was on her way to the crude platform. She seemed flying rather than walking, her small moccasin feet touching the board steps on her toes, her long, black curls flying back over her shoulders. As she gained the top step she pause, breathless, for an instant and smoothed the ruffles of her new red dress with her brown fingers. This was her first appearance in public and a sudden bashfulness seized her. Then regaining her self-control, she ran lightly to the center of the stage and stood beside the old flag, her small figure reaching only half its height as she recited in her clear, childish voice:

"Your flag and my flag, and O, how much it holds!
Your land and my land secure within its folds."

Without finishing the poem she stooped, and lifting the corner of the tattered flag to her lips, kissed it; then turning, she ran swiftly down the steps to her mother's side.

"Well, I'll be blessed!" exclaimed her father. "Who taught her that?"

For an instant there was profound silence, and then a burst of applause resounded throughout the rough frame school room. Stella, embarrassed, hid her face on her mother's shoulder as Libby placed her arm caressingly about the trembling child.

By the time school closed the board had decided to build a sod school house which was to be located half a mile north of the Bateman place. By fall the new building was completed and George Klapper was employed as teacher.

During the next summer a roving band of range cattle, seeking pasture in the valley, took refuge from the blazing sun in the shade of the little sod school house. Playfully they began to rake the corners of the house with their long, sharp horns. That was fun for the cattle, and besides, the fine dust from the dry sod scared away the flies that tormented them. Soon others, seeing the dust flying, joined in the game and horned away the corners and the little sod school house was demolished, burying seats, desk and all under the thatched roof.

Chapter 19

The Move to Sidney

Joe had not fully recovered from the severe attack of rheumatism which almost cost him his life during the winter. As usual, he and Libby talked over the trying situation of living on the farm.

"I don't believe I can stand another winter on the claim," said Joe. "I think it would be better for us all if we moved to Sidney. There I could do inside work of some kind and not be exposed to the cold weather."

"Yes, and I could take in sewing or something," said Libby.

"I had hoped that our next move would be to Oregon," said Joe, "but that would take more money than we could raise."

"We'll have to wait awhile longer for that," said Libby.

"I hear there's gong to be an irrigation project goes in the valley above here within the next few years. If it does go in, we may be able to sell this place for a good price."

"Then we'll have money enough to go on to Oregon," said Libby.

"I may have to ask for a pension," said Joe. "I've always said that I gave my service to Uncle Sam and that I'd never ask for pay for it, but since I was sick last winter I've thought I may have to ask for help."

"You earned all you'll ever get from the government," replied Libby. "I think you'd be wise if you applied for it right away. It may take a long time to get it. You know Dr. Field offered to make out your application that night he was here when you were sick last winter."

"Yes, I know. We'll see," replied Joe.

The ten-acre field of potatoes was planted on the timber claim where potatoes had been planted the year before, but which failed to grow on account of the dry weather.

"I'll take another chance," said Joe. "Maybe they'll do better this year. There was lots of snow last winter and there is more moisture in the ground than there was last summer."

Lizzie and Clara took turns dropping the cut-up pieces of potatoes in the cool furrows as their father turned the black sod over them. It was not long before the sturdy green leaves began to appear in the long rows.

Hay harvest was over and the Kirkpatrick family was planning to move to Sidney. It was October before all preparations could be made and the air already had the tang of winter in it. Joe came in from the stable one day with a troubled look in his brown eyes. "Pete, the brown mule's pretty sick this morning," he told Libby. "Get me the *Mustang* liniment and I'll get the old horse blanket. He seems to have a cold on his lungs. He's shiverin' all over and he can hardly breathe."

Joe and Libby worked over the sick animal most of the day and left him covered with the warm blanket that night, but by next morning Pete lay cold and rigid in his stall, while Jack, the bay mule looked on in wonder.

Joe was able to borrow a horse at the Cedar Creek ranch until he could move to Sidney. It was a subdued and serious family that said good-bye to their friends in the Weir Valley as they took their last look at their sod house which had been home for them for more than a year.

Chapter 20

The Mail that Brought Good Cheer!

It was a clear, sunny day in late October when the pioneer family arrived in Sidney. It took the next three days for them to get settled in their basement apartment in the Haskell's house on the outer edge of town. Joe soon found employment at a lumber yard. At that time Sidney had a garrison of several hundred soldiers. The small town was taxed to the limit to supply the incidental needs of the soldiers which were not supplied by the government. Libby saw her opportunity to get work that she could do at home and it wasn't long before she was busy washing, ironing and repairing the soldiers' clothing. Will had remained at the Tom Wagoner ranch where he had worked the previous summer.

For the first time in their lives the three older girls entered a graded school. Stella fitted perfectly into the second grade, with dainty little Mrs. Carr as her teacher and was happy in her new life. The older girls, Lizzie and Clara, found it more difficult to adjust themselves to the new conditions. They were both placed in the third grade the first day. The next morning Mr. McCoy, principal of the school, asked the two girls to come to his office. With fear and trembling they followed him upstairs to his office where he gave them an oral test. He was a, middle-aged man, kind and considerate with the two frightened new-comers. When the test was finished he assigned Lizzie to the fourth grade and Clara to the third. Both grades were in the same room and were taught by a beautiful, blonde woman named Miss Wilkins who made the two girls welcome and soon they were enjoying their school life.

All went well with the pioneer family until Stella came home one evening broken out with measles. Within a week every child in the family had them. Joe had had the measles, but Libby had not, so it was not surprising that she was next to come down with them. She was very sick for a week or more, but the children were soon able to return to school.

After the fall work was well in hand at the Wagoner ranch Will joined the family in Sidney and found work in the same lumber yard with his father.

Soon after Joe moved to Sidney he went to Dr. Field's office. "When you came out to see me last winter," he began, "you mentioned for me to applying for a pension. I said then that I'd never ask Uncle Sam for a dollar as long as I could work and earn a living and I meant every word of it. Since I had that spell of rheumatism, I find I can't work like I used to. We've moved here to Sidney where I can get an inside job. My expenses are heavy and my wages are not enough to keep us, so I've decided to apply for a pension."

"I think you're wise," said Dr. Field. "I'll give you a physical examination and we'll have the papers made out right away. It may be a year or more before you get your pension. You'll have to have witnesses and that'll take time."

That day the doctor gave him his examination. The application was made out, signed and sealed by a notary and sent to Washington, D.C., and the period of waiting began. He found that his key witness had died some years before and others had moved from their former homes.

The next spring the family moved to a house known as the Borquist house on the opposite side of town so as to be nearer to Joe's work. Will went to work at a big cattle ranch in Wyoming. Clara had her first experience at working at the home of Mr. and Mrs. Eubank. Mr. Eubank was the banker in Sidney. Their daughter Mamie was the only child in the family. Clara learned a great deal about housekeeping that she could not possibly have learned in a sod house such as she had lived in while on the North Platte valley.

Lizzie was her mother's helper and stayed at home. The younger children played through the long summer days after school was out.

There was great excitement in the Weir Valley that summer. It was rumored that an irrigation ditch was to be dug above the Cedar Creek ranch and that the valley land below was to be supplied with water. The surveyors were already at work.

"Now's the time to sell both the preemption and the timber claims," said Joe. "I'll go out and dig the potatoes we planted last spring, if there are any there to dig." He put the sale of the homestead in the hands of a real-estate dealer and went out to dig his potatoes.

"How'd you like to go with me, Clara?" he asked, "and help me dig the potatoes?"

"O, I'd love it!" replied Clara, so bidding goodbye to the Eubank family, she quit her first job and went with her father to dig the potatoes.

There was a fine crop of potatoes. It was surprising that anything could grow so well without cultivation or water. Joe turned back the sod with a borrowed plow as Clara picked up the big, red potatoes that had grown flat between the sod and the solid earth beneath it. The soil had retained enough moisture to make the potatoes grow.

The claim was sold in the fall and the money deposited in the bank to have in case of need, or, perhaps, to take to Oregon, as Joe had promised.

"Let's hope it will take us to Oregon," said Libby.

An epidemic of grip, or flu, struck the country during the latter part of the winter and again, the whole family, except Joe came down with it. The schools were closed for two weeks. Joe had to leave his work and take care of the family. Libby was very ill, and continued to cough long after the children were well and had returned to school.

As Joe walked home from his work one evening and stopping by the Post Office, a large official-looking letter was handed to him. On the upper left hand corner were the words, "*United States Treasury Department, Office of Pensions, Washington, D.C.*" With eager fingers he tore open the envelope and read its contents. Two Government checks were enclosed; one for three hundred dollars and one for twelve dollars. The accompanying note explained that the three hundred dollars was back pension and the twelve dollar check was his pension for the current month.

He hurried home to tell Libby the good news. "Now, we can go to Oregon," he said. "With this and the money we got from the sale of the homestead we'll have enough to pay our way on the train and have some left."

"Yes, the big check will pay our fares," replied Libby, "but twelve dollars a month will be only a drop in the bucket after we get there."

In the same mail was another letter which Joe had overlooked in his haste to open the big envelope. He handed the small letter to Libby. "It is from Sister Lena Clark," said Libby excitedly. "I wonder if anything has happened to them. They haven't written for a long time and anything could happen in that time."

She opened the letter with trembling fingers and read it eagerly. She was always glad to hear from her sisters and especially from Lena who had left Missouri as a young girl and had gone to California to live with a family of old friends.

When her uncle, Austin Leonard, heard that she was living in California, he immediately set out by team from his home near Silverton, Oregon, and brought her to his home to live. She married Cyrus Clark, a young carpenter who lived near her uncle's home and had moved to a farm not far from the little town of Sublimity. They had three children, all girls, and the oldest was about the age of Clara. For several years the two girls had corresponded, and felt that they knew each other very well. Libby's sister seldom wrote, and Libby wondered why Hattie, the oldest girl, had not written this time. It proved that in her last letter Clara had mentioned the fact that if they could manage it they wanted to go to Oregon the following spring. Her aunt Lena had answered the letter, urging them to come as soon as possible.

By a strange coincidence her letter had arrived with the same mail as the letter containing the two checks, which made it possible for the family to realize their long dream of going to Oregon.

Libby read the letter to Joe as the children stood about them, listening. "Lena will be glad to see us," she said, as she finished reading the letter. A fit of coughing seized the frail little woman as she spoke. "I hope this cough gets better before we leave for Oregon," she said.

"The change of climate may do you good," said Joe.

"I hope so," replied Libby, drying her eyes on the corner of her apron. "This cough is getting to be a nuisance."

Chapter 21

On To Oregon! (1890)

School was not yet out, but preparations were being made to make the long trek to Oregon. The bay mule was sold at a good price, and the children hated to part with their old play-fellow, but Jack could not go with them this time, as he had done so often before. The few pieces of furniture were disposed of for what they would bring, all but the big clock, which was packed carefully for shipment and taken with the family. Joe and Will prepared packing boxes while Libby, assisted by Clara and Lizzie, folded garments and packed them away, ready for shipment, while the three younger children darted here and there, trying to help wherever they could. Clothing for the journey was packed in two large suitcases and food to last four days was packed in a large wooden box.

Will had saved enough money to buy a ticket back to Ohio, for he had longed to visit the relatives left behind when the family went to Kansas ten years before. He and Joe went to the ticket office together, Will to buy his ticket to Ohio and Joe to buy tickets for himself and the rest of the family to Oregon. Will started on his journey the next day amid goodbyes and the waving of hands by the family.

It was April 8, 1890, and a snow storm was raging over the wide prairies and swept over the little town of

Sidney in a furious blast. Everything was packed and there was no turning back now, storm or no storm. Joe hired a man from the mill where he had been working to take his wagon with high sideboards to transport his family and the luggage to the railroad station. Boxes and bags were soon stored away in the roomy wagon bed and the five children sat on the boxes while Joe and the driver spread a great tarpaulin over the top of the wagon box. It was dark as night in there, but the children didn't mind. They were too excited about going to Oregon to care if it was dark. Libby and Joe wrapped in their heavy coats, climbed to the seat with the driver, and were soon at the little train station.

Through the blinding storm the train sped until they began the climb towards the Rocky Mountains where the snow suddenly ceased and the train emerged above the clouds and into the clear, sparkling sunshine. The sharp peaks of the Rockies with their snow covered crests loomed above them, silhouetted against the clear, blue sky. It was an inspiring sight and the travelers gazed in wonder at its dazzling beauty. It was the first time the prairie bred family had ever seen high mountains. Libby drew in deep breaths of the invigorating air. It was the first time in weeks that she had been able to take a deep breath without coughing. From that time on, she was free from her nagging cough.

At Green River, Wyoming, the travelers transferred to another train which took them to Pocatello, Idaho. There they saw the first Indians any of them had ever seen. There were big, sturdy bucks with grimy blankets over their shoulders and black hair hanging down behind them in two long braids. There were fat squaws with bright colored kerchiefs tied close about their heads and beaded capes about their brown shoulders. Half a dozen papooses danced near the steps of the coach as trainmen tossed pennies on the frozen ground for them as their small, moccasin feet tapping swiftly and noiselessly on the hard-packed snow of the railroad yard.

Night had fallen when they crossed the Idaho boarder into Oregon so the travelers did not see the broad prairies covered with sage brush. Joe set his watch ahead an hour at Huntington, Oregon, because there they entered the Pacific time zone. They crossed the Cascade Mountains and followed the Columbia River down to Portland.

Such a bedlam of voices greeted their ears as they reached the Central Station! It was the hotel cab drivers calling their hotels.

"Right this way, Mister," shouted a cabby, seizing the suitcase Joe was carrying.

"I am going to the Farmer's Hotel," said Joe, somewhat bewildered. "A fellow on the train recommended it."

"This cab is for that hotel," declared the cabby and the weary family piled into the waiting cab.

The next morning from their hotel window Libby looked across the street and saw the sign, Farmer's Hotel. The cab driver had lied to them and had taken them to another hotel.

Somewhat rested from their long journey they took the first train south to Turner on the Southern Pacific railroad. Spring was in the air. Willows and alders fringed the borders of the Willamette River and grass laid as a soft carpet along its rippling margins. Robins could be seen hopping about among the trees and at the station grounds wherever the train stopped in the broad valley. Orchards were in bloom and farmers were plowing their brown fields. Dark forests of fir and pine trees covered the nearby hills and distant mountains. To the left Mt. Hood loomed in all its snowy glory and to the south of it an occasional glimpse of Mt. Jefferson's shining crest was visible.

The prairie-bred family, starved for the sight of trees and mountains, drank in the beauty of the scenery.

"It's God's country!" exclaimed Joe, as he gazed in wonder at the beautiful landscape.

Past the falls at Oregon City and on to Salem, the state's capital, they sped.

"Only eight more miles and we'll be in Turner," said Joe. "I wonder if Cy will be there to meet us."

"Cousin Hattie said in her last letter that he'd send a bus to meet us," said Lizzie.

Boxes, bundles and suitcases were made ready and the family from Nebraska sat waiting for the whistle to sound.

The bus, drawn by a team of horses and driven by Mr. Thomas was waiting for them carrying them safely over the muddy roads between overhanging hazel and alder bushes, flanked by tall fir trees, to the home of Uncle Cy Clark, six miles east of Turner.

"Here they come!" called Uncle Cy as the bus turned in at his gate. Aunt Lena and their three young daughters; Hattie, Kate and Wilda gathered about him on the front porch to greet them.

"Glad to see you!" exclaimed Cy, wringing Joe's hand. "Come on in! We're waitin' dinner for you."

"That's fine!" replied Joe. "We've not had a square meal since we left Sidney."

Libby and her sister Lena greeted each other with tears in their eyes, while the three Clark girls and the new cousins shook hands shyly.

"Well, Joe," said Lena, as she clasped his hand, "your dream has come true at last!"

"Yes, thanks to the Lord," replied Joe fervently. "We've been on our way to Oregon ever since we left Ohio more that ten years ago. We've finally reached the Promised Land at last!"

Ware's Guide to Emigrants

SIX MONTH'S SUPPLIES NEEDED FOR OREGON TRAIL JOURNEY

Recommended Supplies for Family of Four:

- 800 POUNDS FLOUR
- 200 POUNDS LARD
- 25 POUNDS SALT & PEPPER
- 200 POUNDS BEANS
- 700 POUNDS BACON
- 100 POUNDS DRIED FRUIT
- 75 POUNDS COFFEE
- 2,000 POUNDS TOTAL

★ No more than 2400 pounds should be taken in one wagon.
THIS CAUSED MANY FAMILIES TO TAKE MORE THAN ONE WAGON.

COOKING UTENSILS
GUNS & AMMO
EATING UTENSILS
CLOTHING & PERSONAL ITEMS
*FURNITURE (IF WEIGHT AND ROOM ALLOWED)

*NOTE: MOST FURNITURE ITEMS WERE EVENTUALLY DISCARDED TO LIGHTEN THE HEAVY LOAD AS THE ANIMALS WORE OUT AND DIED.

ANIMALS NEEDED
4 to 6 OXEN AT $25.00 EACH
3 TEAMS OR 6 OXEN WERE TYPICAL
OR:
8 to 10 MULES AT $75.00 EACH

[OXEN WERE PREFERRED SINCE THEY WERE MUCH GENTLER, STEADIER AND IN CASE OF DIRE NEED COULD BE EATEN.]

KIRKPATRICK FAMILY

Elizabeth and Joseph Kirkpatrick

AUMSVILLE, OREGON 1898

Back row from left – Eddie, Willie, Clara, Lizzie,
Front row from left – Stella,
Joseph, Elizabeth, Hattie

Made in the USA
Monee, IL
18 August 2024

64007867R00090